Room 22 Revisited

or

Mare o' t'Same
(More of the Same)

H. G. Wills

ARTHUR H. STOCKWELL LTD
Torrs Park, Ilfracombe, Devon, EX34 8BA
Established 1898
www.ahstockwell.co.uk

British Library Cataloguing-in-Publication Data.
A catalogue record for this book is available
from the British Library.

By the same author:
The Best Kept Secrets of the Western Marches

ISBN 978-0-7223-4649-5
Printed in Great Britain by
Arthur H. Stockwell Ltd
Torrs Park   Ilfracombe
Devon EX34 8BA

CONTENTS

ACKNOWLEDGEMENTS

The following people and organisations have been extremely helpful in the production of both books – *The Best Kept Secrets of the Western Marches* and *Room 22 Revisited* – mostly in providing detailed and background information, but also in giving advice and support:

1) English Heritage:
   i)   Andrew Davison – Principal Inspector for Ancient Monuments.
   ii) Liz Page – Historic Properties Director (North).
   iii) Carole Keltie – General Manager of Hadrian's Wall.
   iv) Mark Douglas – Job Property Curator Team Leader in York.
2) The Victoria and Albert Museum: Dr Paul Williamson.
3) The Royal College of Arms: Robert Noel – Lancaster Herald.
4) The Towton Battlefield Association: Graham Darbyshire.
5) Naworth Castle: Philip Howard.

There have also been a host of others behind the scenes offering encouragement, taking photographs and reading initial manuscripts – some of their advice was actually taken. These unsung heroes include John Robinson, Ken Fryer, Paul and Mark Haycock, Dr David Harle, Dr Moira Brimacombe, Steve Matthews, Rory Stewart, M.P., and Melvyn Bragg.

ILLUSTRATIONS AND FAMILY TREES

Front Cover: An image of the North Wall.
Back Cover: An illuminated 'C'.

Carlisle Castle
(circa 1550)

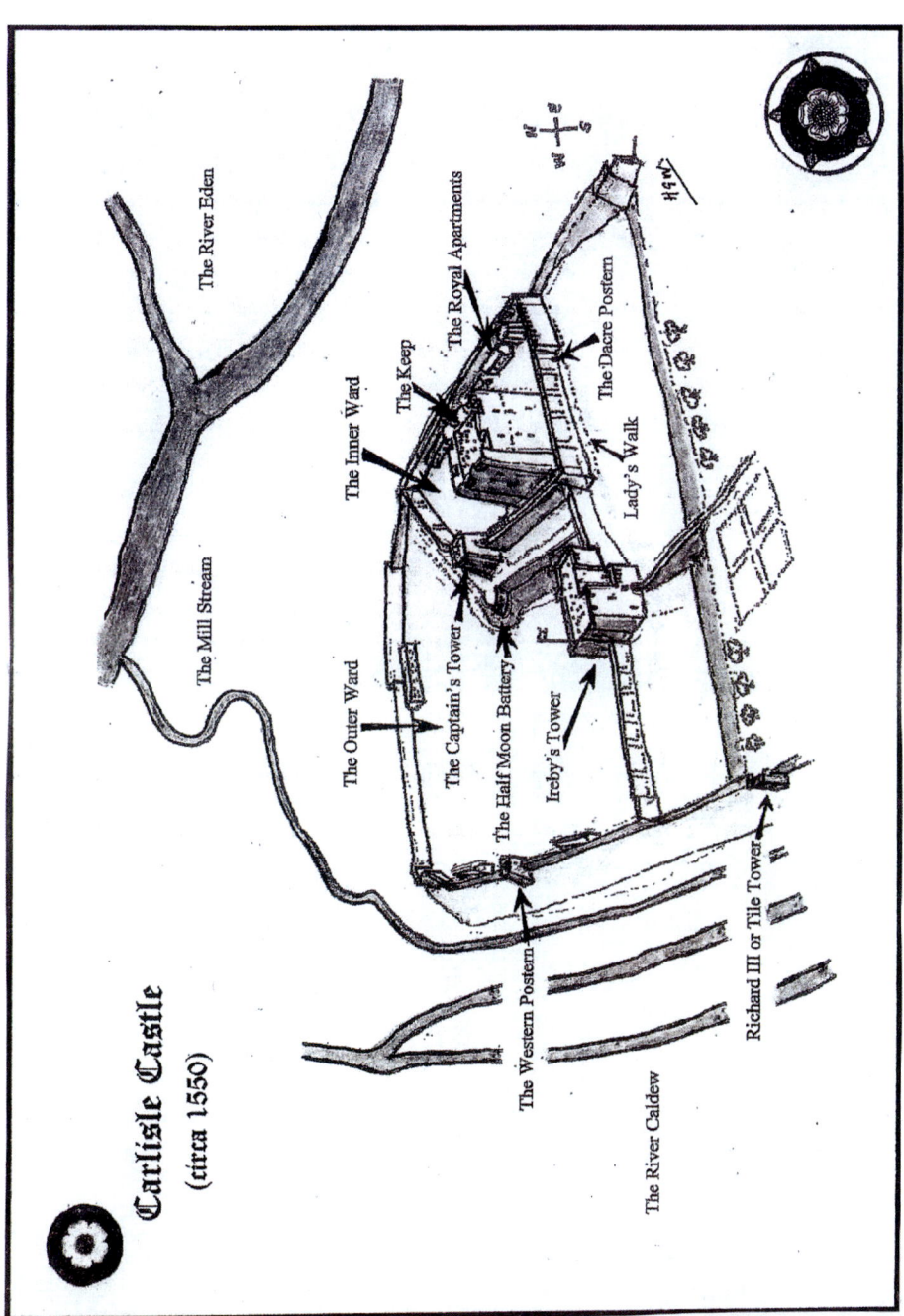

The River Eden

The Mill Stream

The Outer Ward

The Inner Ward

The Keep

The Royal Apartments

The Dacre Postern

Lady's Walk

The Captain's Tower

The Half Moon Battery

Ireby's Tower

The Western Postern

Richard III or Tile Tower

The River Caldew

The Keep of Carlisle Castle –A View from the North-Eastern Aspect.
Room 22

The Second Floor Layout.
Room 17.
Room 21.
Room 22.
Room 23.
A Section of the Keep through all Floors.
Room 17.
Rooms 22& 23

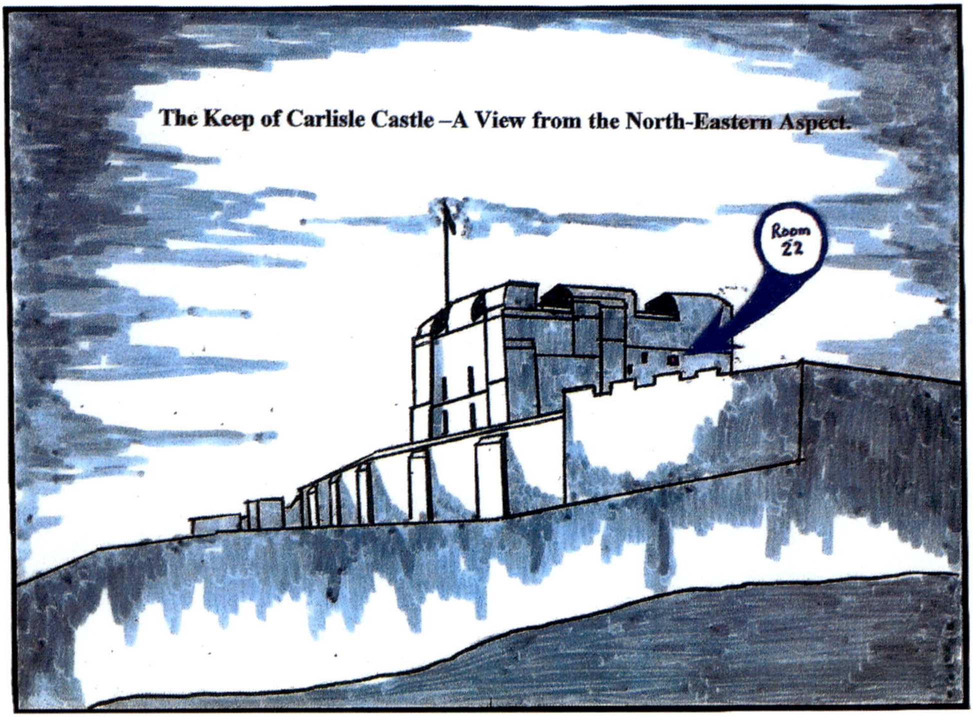

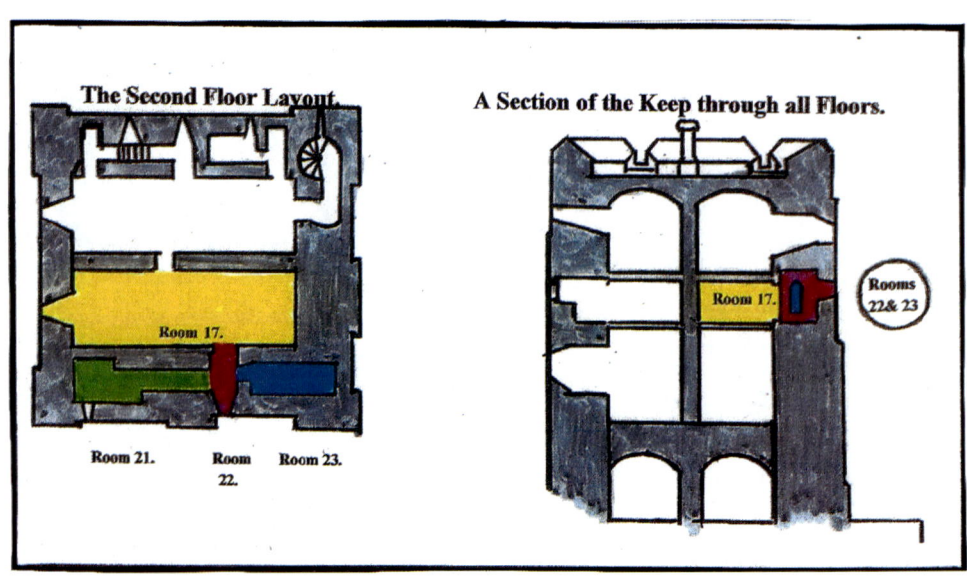

INTRODUCTION

In July of 2015, shortly after Arthur H. Stockwell Ltd printed the first copy of *The Best Kept Secrets of the Western Marches*, I began to reappraise the pictograms in Room 22 – reassessing the images and looking for alternative explanations in anticipation of being asked to justify my conclusions.

Block 26 posed a very real problem. It clearly showed Dacre, Percy and Roos family badges and the only connection between them seemed to be that important members of those families had all fought on the Lancastrian side at the 'Bloody Battle of Towton' in 1461. I wasn't entirely sure of the identities of all of the combatants and I had in addition some niggling doubts as to when this commemorative plaque could have been carved. Staring at the screen, as if in hope of inspiration, I drew a complete blank . . . and then looked away. It was at that moment – with the laptop screen at a slightly more acute angle, as I leaned back – that I spotted something that I had never seen before.

At first, they just seemed like faint disconnected lines, just visible beneath the three Percy fusils. And then, like one of those illusory drawings with hidden secondary images, I saw it . . . the faint but just discernible incomplete outline of a headless deer. It was just like one of the many stick-like images in the panoramic hunting scene, which were probably the earliest images to be carved on the walls of Room 22.

A month or so earlier, I had discovered by sheer chance another faint outline on one of the unnumbered blocks on the North Wall – a large four-petal flower. One discovery was a nuisance, but two demanded attention. For the next few hours I reviewed my collection of over 100 photographs – each one enlarged and patiently scanned in detail. In the end I found another twenty-five of these outline images.

Why had they been overlooked? At first I could find no plausible reason . . . and then the penny dropped! Shortly afterwards, I began to draw them all and try to make sense of this bag of old pennies.

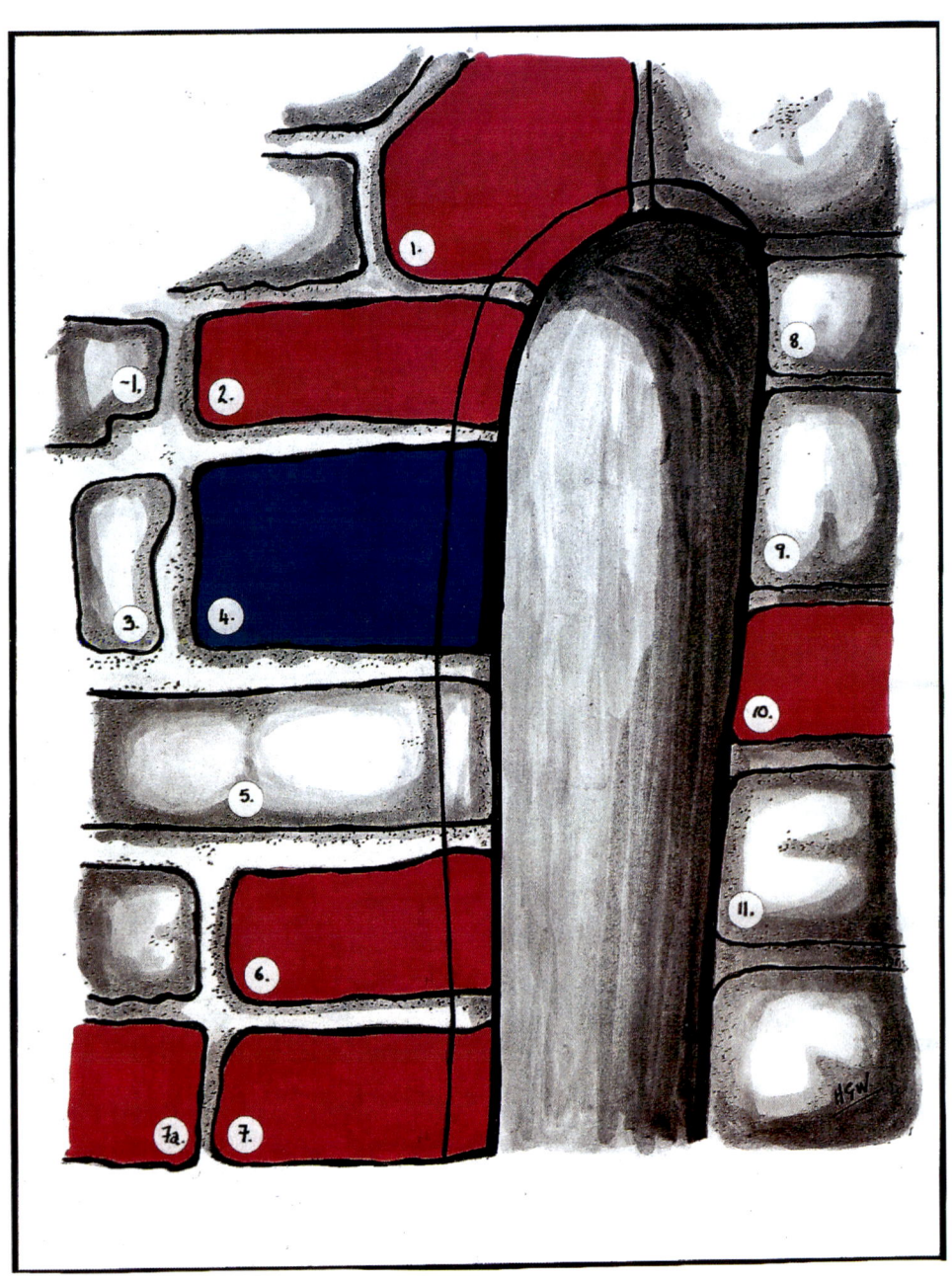

The North Wall.

14

The East Wall and window.

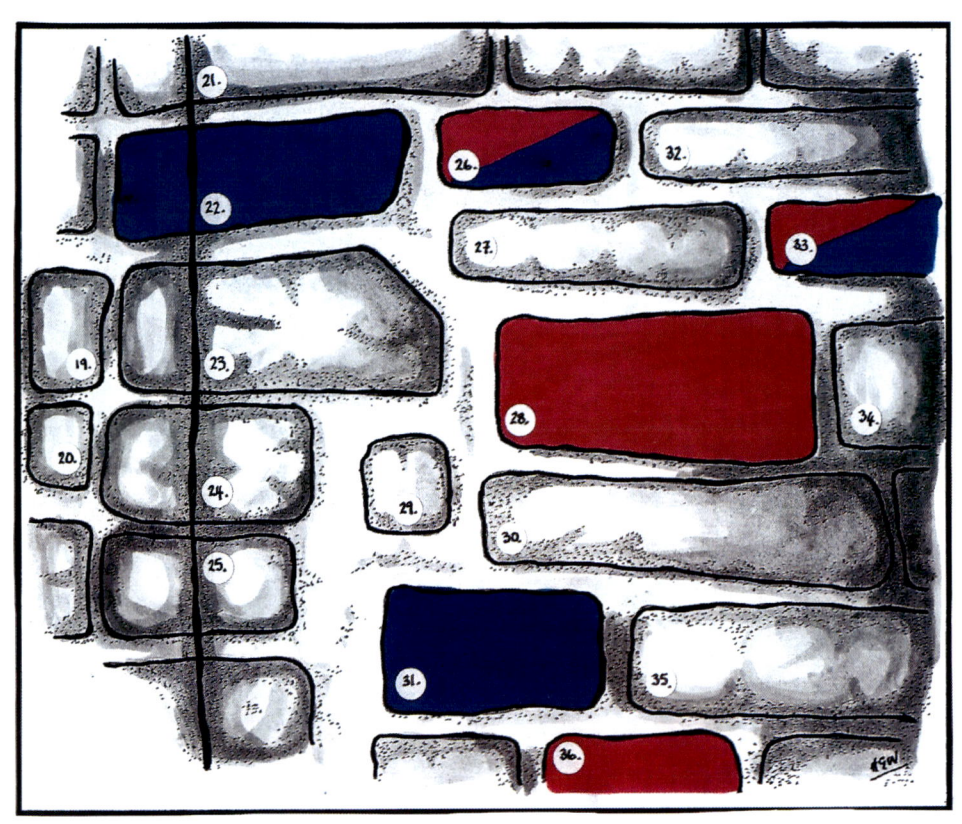

The South Wall.

PART 1 – THE OUTLINE IMAGES

It seems inconceivable that nearly thirty images could have been missed during the numerous detailed inspections of the photographs of the blocks in Room 22.

Three certainly were not and, not to put too fine a point on it, had been ignored! Three arrows on three different blocks were clearly later additions to the original carvings. The first can be seen to the lower right of the image of a collared white hart on the upper part of Block 1. The second is visible in the central part of the cartouche depicting St George and the dragon on Block 2. The last is on top of a deer on the extreme left of Block 33.

All three are probably modern graffiti and could have been carved by anyone, at any time, by someone who thought one more missile amongst a plethora of others would never be noticed. Actually, as it turned out, these three were – being so totally out of context with regard to the images they were carved on or next to. Indeed, it is quite possible there are a few more arrows and arrowheads with a similar parentage.

As for the other 'missed images', some turned out to just be of the type previously described as over-carved images – ones upon which later images were superimposed leaving only remnants of the former.

However, well over 60% of the 'missed images' fall into a new category – one which might better be described as 'outline images' and there seems to be a very good reason why they have not come to light before now.

They were never intended to be seen as finished images and were just preliminary, partial and faint outline sketches, which were abandoned well before completion.

This assertion is not an excuse for a massive oversight and the proof lies in three parts:

1) Firstly, many of these carvings are so faint that they can barely be seen on photographic images – even when enlarged – and would

17

have been virtually invisible in the dim natural light of Room 22.
2) Secondly, most of these images are incomplete – some just a collection of disconnected scratches, which only merge into recognisable shapes after close and prolonged inspection.
3) Lastly, most of them are on blocks on peripheral rows and, as such, might well have been the last images of a particular theme to have been embarked upon. They were and still are images well out of the line of sight of a casual observer and have to be carefully searched for to be seen.

Another factor seems very important with regard to these images. Their faintness and state of incompletion, when viewed next to the completed images, hints at something that has not been alluded to before – that there must have been a sequence of stages involved in the carving of most or all of the images. The outline images must therefore be just an early stage in what must have been a carving process.

Thus the skills employed by these talented but amateur craftsmen have really been underestimated – perhaps because, as people, they have been described as simple, ordinary, illiterate medieval peasants. However, it is too simplistic to believe the carvers just quickly knocked off their pictures in a casual, carefree and unplanned manner on the surface of any old sandstone block within reach. Although not professional stonemasons, they would have known trained artisans in the city – like those working at the cathedral – who could easily have given our carvers the odd tip or two about working on stone surfaces. Perhaps there was even a shared knowledge amongst others employed in the castle, as to how such images could be created.

So what might this carving process have involved?

1) Firstly, the choice of a suitable block – one well illuminated, reasonably flat and at an appropriate height for carving. All pretty obvious, some might say, but a number of factors need to be taken into account – such as:
   a) When the best light would shine into Room 22 through its small east window and whether it was a sunny or a cloudy day.
   b) The cost or availability of artificial illumination.
   c) The fact that the average height of a medieval man was five feet seven inches and thus blocks at eye level – just over five feet from the floor – would have been ideal.

2) Slightly uneven-surfaced blocks would have posed few problems, as the soft sandstone could easily have been smoothed over with a hard flat stone from the riverbed of the nearby Eden.
3) The next stage would have been to draw the outline of the proposed image. Charcoal would have been readily at hand – even partially burnt twigs from a brazier could have served as a drawing tool.
4) Once drawn, the outline would have been carefully, but initially quite superficially, engraved into the surface of the stone.
5) Subsequent and deeper cuts would have followed, until a satisfactory outline image had been produced.
6) Then the detail features would have been added.
7) The area around the image might then have been scraped away to give the Carving a more three-dimensional appearance.
8) Finally, a surround or cartouche might have been carved out to set off the finished design.

To some all of the above might seem to be fanciful, but it would have been a very logical way to produce carvings on soft sandstone . . . and, in my opinion, well within the capacity of our medieval ancestors, who although illiterate were not stupid or lacking in manual dexterity.

Another point worth considering is that the above process would have taken time. That being so, it seems likely that those in authority in the castle might have turned a blind eye to what was going on in Room 22, after the Earliest Carvings had been produced – see Part 2. Indeed, considering the number of Dacre scallops on the walls of that room, wardens and governors of that name might well have encouraged further carving by men brought with them from Naworth during their tenure of office.

So, what do the outline images look like? The following images are offered as drawings, as even the best printed photographs are far too faint to reveal satisfactory images.

The drawings are shown as combination images of outlines and reconstructed images – ones which would have existed had the carver finished carving them. The faint outline image – all that we can see today – is seen as a fine black outline. The reconstructed part of the completed image is drawn as a thicker red outline and the body of the image is filled in with crimson. The blocks and surrounding images have thick black outlines and are shaded with a grey wash to enhance and make the reconstructed outline images stand out.

* * * * *

To identify the location of each numbered block, see the three drawings showing the North, East and South Walls at the beginning of this chapter. They are colour-coded as follows:

1) Red for numbered blocks with outline images.
2) Blue for numbered blocks with pictograms – see later in Part 4.
3) Red/blue for numbered blocks with both of the above.
4) Grey for other numbered blocks, which have images, but which do not fall into any of the above categories.

* * * * *

1) Block 1:
High up on the North Wall – on the left-hand side of the doorway to Room 23 – is a large block with a number of images, one being a white hart with a crown-like collar, the livery badge of both Richard II of Bordeaux and Henry V, although some believe it to be one used by both the Stanley and Greystoke families. Whatever the case, just to its right is one of the three arrows mentioned earlier as additional and unrelated later graffiti.

2) Block 2:
A second arrow can be seen on the extreme left of Block 2 – right in the middle of a depiction of St George killing a dragon. It is so out of place in this cameo, it can only be a latter addition.

3) Block 2:
On the extreme right of Block 2 is a large black-painted padlock attached to a heavy-duty metal ring, which is probably a 19th-century arrangement for securing the door to Room 23. Beneath the ring is the tail of a medieval serpent and above that appears to be a crudely carved horizontal grid. Just visible within the grid is the face and upper body of a man with outstretched arms – in a crucifixion-like pose. This presumably was going to be another image of Christ on the Cross.

4) Block 6:
Three blocks beneath Block 2 is another heavy-duty metal ring and just visible beneath that are the faint carvings of what are almost certainly the protruding fore and rear legs of a deer facing to the left.

North Wall.

Block 1.

Block 2.

21

North Wall.

Block 2.

Block 6.

22

North Wall.

Block 7.

Block 7a.

North Wall.

Block 10.

Block 10.

24

East Wall.

Block 13.

Block 14.

Block 17a.

5) Block 7:

Beneath and to the left of the legs on Block 6 is a large blank-faced man with long legs and 'curly feet'. Beneath him is a finely carved large and virtually complete Dacre scallop.

6) Block 7a:

To the left of Block 7 is Block 7a and on it, taking up most of the surface of this fairly large block is the faint outline of a large four-petal flower. Fully detailed but smaller flowers of this type can be seen on the East and South Walls. They have been described as 'white Yorkist roses', but generally roses especially the Tudor rose have five petals. However, according to the heralds at the Royal College of Arms, heraldic roses with four or five petals are equally common – the former may be of the wild hedgerow rather than the garden variety.

7) Block 10:

On the right side of the doorway to Room 23 is Block 10, which features an ornate 'white Yorkist rose' (red roses were never used as symbols during the so-called Wars of the Roses). To its left is a carving of the 'Wheel of Fortune', often mistaken for Catherine's wheel.

St Catherine of Alexandria was beheaded on the orders of Emperor Maxentius around AD 310, whose original orders were that she should be 'broken on a spiked wheel'. The latter fell to pieces when coming into contact with the saint, who much later was seen by Joan of Arc in her visions. For reasons which are not quite clear, the name 'Catherine's wheel' became associated with a modern firework.

The 'Wheel of Fortune' was a common medieval symbol depicting life's vagaries of luck and misfortune.

Between the wheel and the rose are two arrowheads, which are almost completely obscured by both of these carvings and, as such, should really be considered as over-carved, rather than outline images.

8) Block 10:

Also on the same block but much further to the left – next to a half-carved upper torso of a crucified man – are the faintest of outlines of the neck and head of a doe.

9) Block 13:

On the left-hand side of the window on the East Wall are two completed images of deer – a fawn and its mother. Just above these are two other deer – presumably does.

10) Block 14:

On the other side of the window and slightly higher up the wall than Block 13 is Block 14, which has on it a confusing and complex arrangement of fine linear scratches, which, when enlarged and scrutinised, reveal the faint outlines of four images – two arrowheads, a horse and a hunter.

11) Block 17a:

This block is high up on the East Wall, just inside the corridor leading to Room 21. In the dim light the faint and incomplete outline of a doe can just be discerned.

12) Block 21a:

On the lintel above the doorway of the corridor leading to Room 21 is the incomplete outline of a knight's head, wearing a sallet-type helmet with its visor raised. Larger versions of similar images can be seen on Blocks 30 and 34 on the right-hand side of the South Wall and all three may well be depictions of Thomas Dacre, 1st Baron Dacre of Greystoke and 2nd Baron Dacre of Gillesland. This would date Block 21a's carving to around 1520.

13) Block 26:

This image of a headless deer on Block 26 on the South Wall is the one which precipitated the entire search for all of the other outline images and came to light, as discussed earlier, by pure chance.

This over-carved deer is one of the many Earliest Carvings in the panoramic hunting scene and as such predates the pictogram of badges by 300 years – both will be discussed in detail later.

14) Block 28:

This block is situated on the South Wall – on the extreme right and in the middle row. The outline image can be found just to the right of a cartouche containing a Greystoke stag's head and consists of the crudest example of a Dacre scallop seen in Room 22.

15) Block 33:

This block is just above the previous one – Block 28 – and shows two images. One can be seen on top of a doe and is the third arrow in the trio of unrelated and later additions. The other image is just below the doe and is the third of three small lions or lion cubs – the other two being on Block 28 and whose significance is obscure.

Block 21a.

29

South Wall.

Block 26.

Blocks 28 and 33.

South Wall.

Block 33.

Block 36.

31

A wall beneath the Captain's Tower.

The lintel above the Dacre Postern Gate.

Naworth Castle.

16) Block 33:

Also on the same block are three other faint carvings:

Firstly, another heart can been seen associated with the figure which may be a depiction of the Black Douglas. This third heart is slightly different in shape to the other two; fainter in outline, more elongated and situated on top of the knight's crested helmet. It makes no sense to carve an image in such a position and may well be a much later addition.

However, it helps to keep an open mind with regard to these Carvings. The complex story relating to Sir James Douglas and the silver casket containing Robert the Bruce's heart will be related in detail later in Part 4 and may offer a plausible explanation for this third heart.

The next image is very faint and consists of a small Carving of the neck and head of a deer – seen just to the left of the Black Douglas.

The final image is hard to make out and looks a little like a bone – a tibia or possibly a humerus!

17) Block 36:

This block is in the bottom row of blocks on the South Wall – towards the right-hand side and just below and to the right of Block 31, which depicts the fox and two birds. The three deer are very faintly outlined and are very easily missed.

18) The Captain's Tower:

On the left-hand wall beneath the Captain's Tower, looking outwards to the castle's car park, is a rather dirty stone block in the centre of the wall – about halfway up. It shows a number '1321' beneath a very chunkily carved fleur-de-lis. Just to the left of these two Carvings appear to be the beginnings of two other fleurs-de-lis.

(As shall be seen in the last chapter, there are more Carvings opposite the above – on the right-hand wall.)

19) The Dacre Postern Gate:

The three extremely weather-beaten Dacre scallops on an equally worn shield – depicting the Dacre coat of arms – is not really a new finding. It has already been described, but to date no representation of its image has been offered. It can just be seen on the lintel above the Dacre Postern Gate at the end of Lady's Walk, which runs from the bridge just outside of Ireby's Tower to the city wall.

Lady's Walk is said to have been used by Mary Queen of Scots, when she was Elizabeth I's guest in the castle in the summer of 1568.

The Dacre Postern Gate may have been named after Ranulph Dacre,

1st Baron Dacre and Warden of the Western Marches between 1333 and 1336, who is said to have ordered its construction.

20) Naworth Castle:

The home of the Dacre family and later that of the Howard family has previously been described as having its own carved stag – albeit the crudest depiction of such an animal and consisting of a collection of connected straight lines.

By comparison, the stick-like images in Room 22 are works of art and have little or nothing to do with the Naworth stag, which, as it happens, does not stand alone and has next to it:

An equally crude carving of a doe beneath the stag.

A strange double-diamond shape.

A possible shield-like shape with a cross on its surface.

It would be extremely convenient, if the carvings at Naworth were of the same standard as those in Carlisle, but they are not. The wooden Dacre Beasts, now in the Victoria and Albert Museum, may well have been produced by the same stonemason, who left the Dacre Bull, two Vaux Gryphons and two Greystoke Dolphins on the South Wall of Room 22, but he had absolutely nothing to do with the Naworth deer.

* * * * *

As a Parthian shot, before leaving the outline images, is there anything more one could deduce from the images of the deer in this category? As partially prepared images on such peripheral sites, it is possible, that they were the last ones in the panoramic hunting scene to have been begun and, perhaps, were discontinued when the reason for their creation ended i.e. on the death or end of tenure of the person, who ordered them carved in the first place. (See later in Part 2, 'More Thoughts on the Earliest Carvings'.)

Gargoyles and other beasties.

One of the earliest of medieval images.

PART 2 – MORE THOUGHTS ON THE EARLIEST CARVINGS

Although the theory behind which Carvings might have been the earliest to have been created in Room 22 was discussed in some detail in *The Best Kept Secrets of the Western Marches*, there still seems to be some scepticism about the propositions offered there.

Using a slightly unconventional approach and adopting a different perspective with the aid of a number of new drawings, the previous hypothesis will be given a new lease of life. Additionally, the discovery of the sixteen missed or outline images of deer and arrowheads – as discussed in Part 1 – gives an even greater impetus to the arguments previously offered.

* * * * *

Forgetting for the moment everything relating to the Carvings, as we know them, on the walls and door of Room 22, let us envisage a situation where we are staring at a room devoid of any Carvings whatsoever. Let us imagine we are looking over the shoulder of the first carver, who is about to cut his first image on the surface of one of those easily worked-on red sandstone blocks.

(Let us also not only disregard completely the date of this action, but also give the carver carte blanche to carve whatever he wants to and wherever he wants to in Room 22.)

So, faced with two of the most promising surfaces – the North and the South Wall – where would our carver have begun his labour of love? Two factors would have governed his decision.

The first would undoubtedly have been light. Room 22 has only a small window on the East Wall, which gives of its best light in the mornings – and not that much either – even on fairly rare sunny days. Additionally, it should be noted that after midday the light would have been much weaker and more diffuse.

39

The second factor he would take into account would have been the height from the floor which he would have found most practical for carving – i.e. eye level or thereabouts. Bearing in mind the average medieval man would have been five feet seven inches tall – this would have been at around sixty-three inches from floor level.

The first two drawings in a series of thirteen entitled 'The Earliest Carvings' show the North and South Walls as they would have appeared without any Carvings whatsoever on them. The two yellow areas indicate the surfaces best illuminated from the small east window – the North Wall from the right and the South Wall from the left. The darker yellow ellipse would have been where the strongest light would have fallen and the lighter yellow ellipse where it was a little weaker. The rest of the blocks would have been poorly lit – even in the mornings. These two areas, oddly enough, also correspond with the best height for carving on – for our average medieval man, that is!

These yellow areas should be seen as the optimal sites for the first carver to begin working on. How many Carvings might have formed the first batch is for the moment irrelevant, as is the time when the second carver began his endeavours. Carvers followed carvers, until all of the best areas were covered with images. Later carvers would have had to work on poorly lit and slightly out-of-reach areas, but eventually most of the surface of the walls would have been covered with Carvings.

Subsequent carvers would have been faced with a dilemma – there being no available sites on which to place their creations. They could either have abandoned the idea completely . . . or done what the first carver did – use the optimal sites in terms of height and light – the yellow areas. Of course, this would have meant carving on top of earlier images and perhaps even completely obliterating them.

However, it is doubtful if he would have cared a jot about destroying the artistic work of people who may have been dead for decades. Our budding artist would simply have ignored what was already there and carved his images on top of the existing ones. And so it went on, until the myriad of mixed themes and over-carvings evolved into the collage of images we see today.

The East Wall has much fewer Carvings and for whatever reason was not so popular with the carvers. The door is covered with images – but there are no over-carvings on its surface, as technically this is virtually impossible to do on wood without creating deep irregular holes.

The next four drawings show in cartoon-like form what the door and North, East and South Walls look like today. This format has been chosen as no panoramic photographs are available and the style of the drawings is in keeping with the medieval imagery.

THE

EARLIEST

CARVINGS

North Wall without any Carvings.

South Wall without any Carvings.

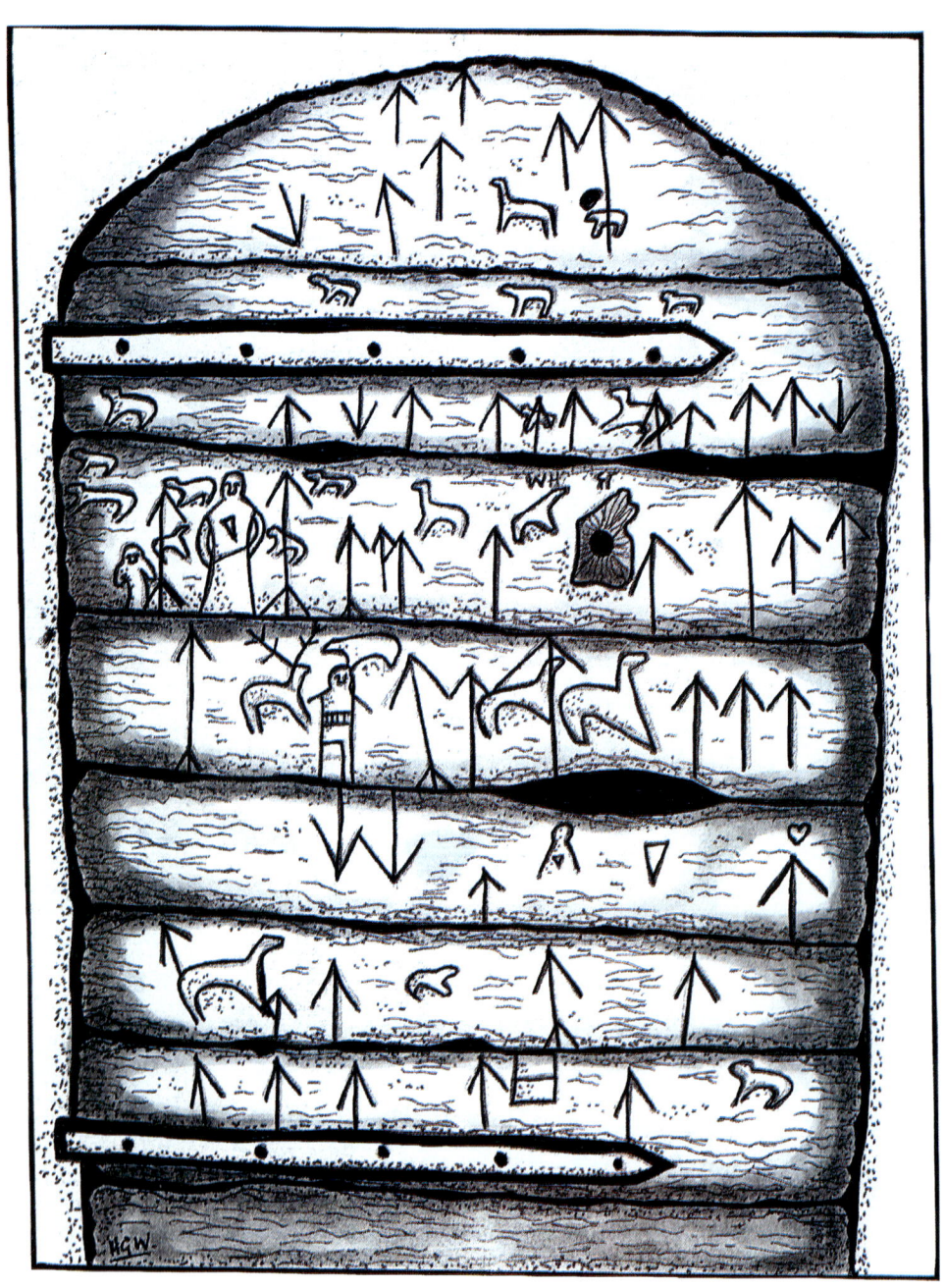

Door fully carved.

44

North Wall fully carved.

45

East Wall fully carved.

46

South Wall fully carved.

47

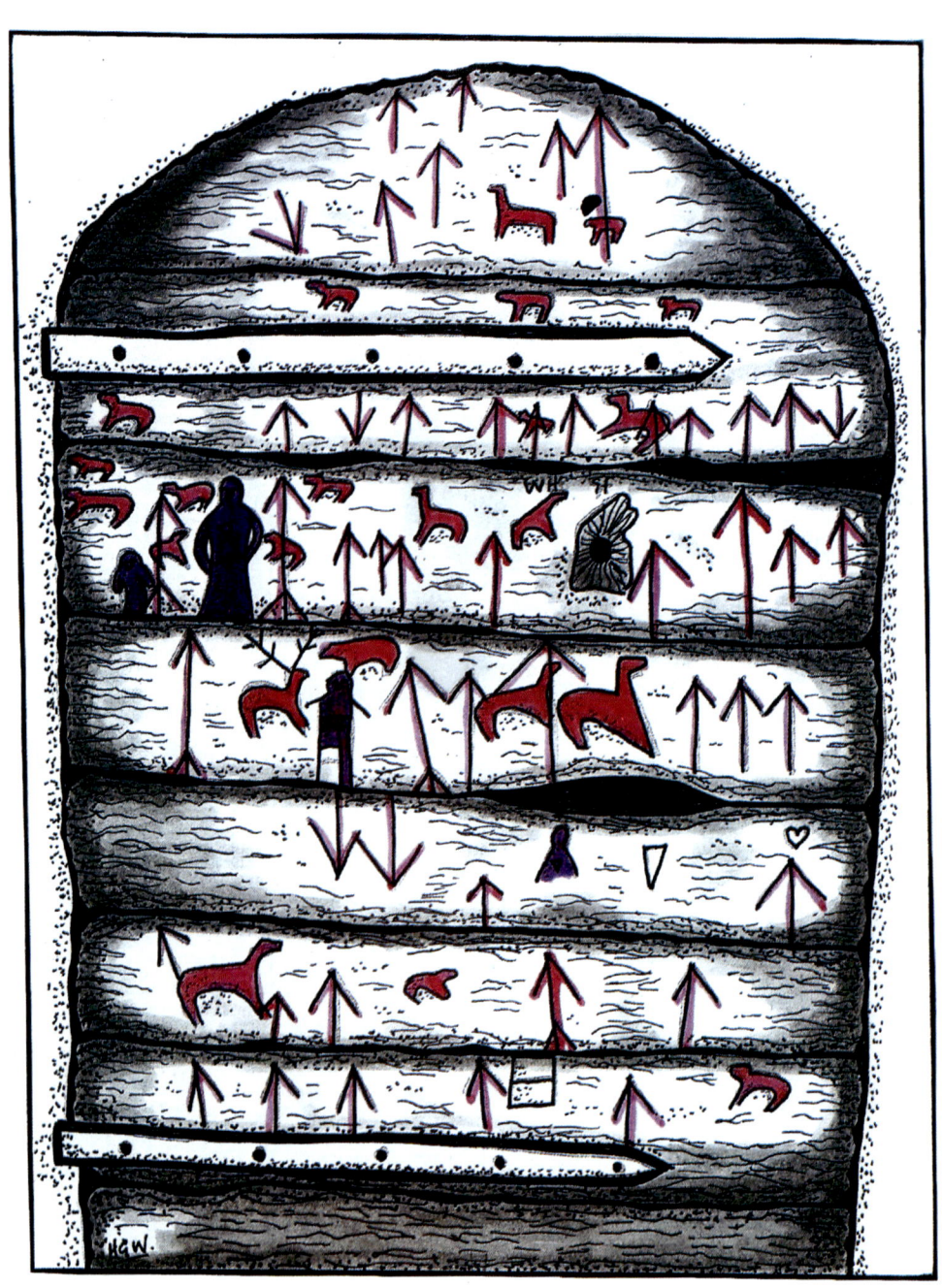

Door with the Earliest Carvings.

48

North Wall with the Earliest Carvings.

49

East Wall with the Earliest Carvings.

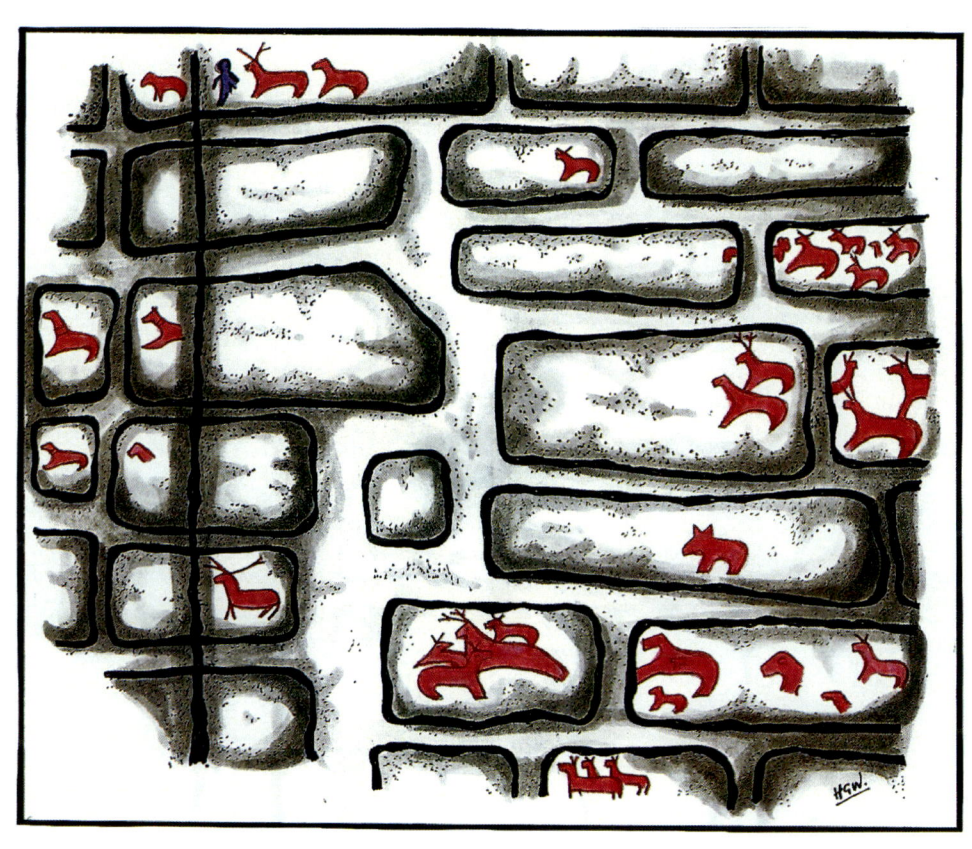

South Wall with the Earliest Carvings.

North Wall with the Earliest Carvings in the best light.

52

South Wall with the Earliest Carvings in the best light.

The South Wall of Room 22 and what might have been.

The task of identifying which images belong to the group labelled as the Earliest Carvings is only marginally helped by having an understanding of what the individual Carvings actually mean. Unfortunately, few of the Carvings are date-specific – even those showing armour have only a thirty-to-fifty-year spectrum of accuracy.

The helmeted knights, heraldic badges associated with the so-called Wars of the Roses and, of course, the Dacre Beasts can all be eliminated from the search, as they clearly belong to the 15th and 16th centuries. However, that still leaves about 90% of the images unaccounted for.

Clearly, a new technique must be employed to find this elusive 'earliest' group – one which relies more on understanding the carving process and not on any knowledge of medieval artefacts.

So, what would help us identify this group? A number of factors need to be taken into account:

1) The images should have a recognisable common theme, so that they can be differentiated from Carvings with different themes.
2) It would be helpful if these images were grouped together, but individual images with the same theme could be seen separated from these groups.
3) It would also make this group's identification simpler if there were sufficient numbers of images with the same theme, as it is easier to work with large numbers than small ones.
4) Over-carving is, perhaps, the most important deciding factor in determining which of the Carvings came first, as if one image is seen to be carved on top of another, the former can only have been carved after the latter.

Thus, with these four factors in mind – of themes, of groupings, of numbers and of over-carving time-relationships – we must scan the walls and door and look for the elusive Earliest Carvings.

As it turns out, the search is comparatively easy, as there is a group of eighty-five images covering the whole of the inner surface of the wooden door between Rooms 17 and 22. They consist of deceptively simple Carvings of stick-like images of stags, does, fawns, hunting dogs, horses, hunters, arrowheads and arrows. Similar images can also be found on the three walls, where over-carving helps to confirm our choice. Thus, the Earliest Carvings form what might aptly be described as a panoramic hunting scene.

Having found which images were most likely to have been the Earliest

Carvings, it would be intriguing to envisage what Room 22 would have looked like when only they adorned the walls and door.
The number involved is around 130, i.e.:

1) Those, which are clearly visible = 100.
2) Those belonging to the rediscovered group of reconstructed fragmentary parts of over-carved deer = 14.
3) Those belonging to the outline-image group = 16.

The next four drawings show what we can prove or perhaps can speculate as to what existed when the Earliest Carvings were the only ones on view:

1) The door is covered with hunting images.
2) The North Wall has a number of deer on the right-hand side of the doorway, in addition to a number of Carvings on the left-hand side, which might have been carved shortly after the earliest images. There is, however, a suspiciously empty area in the centre left-hand side of the doorway – above these three soldiers.
3) The East Wall shows deer on both sides of the window, but is otherwise quite unremarkable.
4) The South Wall has thirty-three images relating to the hunting scene, but what is evident – even more so than on the North Wall – is the central void, where no hunting images can be seen.

If we now lay the yellow ellipses on top of these hunting images on both the North and South Walls, the voids become even more obvious and raise the question that if such areas were originally looked upon as the optimal areas on which to carve the Earliest Carvings – why are they now not in evidence?
The answer is simple. They were once carved on such surfaces, but early images are no longer visible, because they have been over-carved and obliterated out of existence by later images. They are lost forever. If this is true, and it seems most likely, then the number of images belonging to the panoramic hunting scene must have been much greater than 130.
The central area on the South Wall might well have been the centrepiece of this panoramic hunting scene – with numerous mounted hunters with their packs of hounds chasing fleeing deer across the wall from right to left. Thus, the number of images in this 360-degree tableau could well have been nearer 200 than 150! It must have looked

Rediscovered images on Block 31.

Rediscovered images on Block 33.

quite impressive, but the number of images on this scale raises more questions than it offers answers.

The main one is why would anyone carve up to 200 images – spending day after day working on stone block after stone block and on wooden panel after wooden panel? What would have been the motivation behind this almost Herculean endeavour? Equally, as all of these images seem so similar, it looks as if only one person was involved in the task at hand.

However, before we can speculate on the answer to this question, another one demands answering. Would any old Thomas, Richard or Henry have been allowed to carve anything without permission on the internal walls of the keep of Carlisle Castle . . . a royal Border fortress?

I think the answer to that is – "No!" Such an activity would not only have been deemed unacceptable but would have warranted severe punishment. So why and how did these images come into existence?

Perhaps that first carver began his artistic journey without permission and without anyone else knowing what he was up to. However, such an activity could not have gone unnoticed for long. Inevitably, our carver would have eventually been caught red-handed and, doubtless, been dragged before the governor of the castle for his ruling on this serious offence.

There could only have been one of two outcomes to such a meeting:

1) Firstly, the governor, infuriated by the crimes of the grovelling peasant before him, ordered the offending graffiti to be erased and the guilty man severely punished. As the images are still on view today, this could not have happened!

2) The second scenario is that the carver was mildly reprimanded by the governor and then given a surprising offer. Seemingly, the governor liked the images so much that he wanted more of the same carved – in fact he wanted the whole of Room 22 decorated with what would eventually turn out to be a panoramic hunting scene.

The above seems quite plausible, but another question now needs answering. Granted that the governor liked the images so much he wanted more produced, presumably in a room where he could see them on a regular basis, why would he have wanted them carved on the door and walls of Room 22. Today, it is just a small and insignificant room on the second floor of the keep, well out of the way of things.

However, between 1135 and 1172 it was part of the governor's apartment suite, which consisted of Room 21 (the oratory), Room 22 (a small side room/corridor), Room 23 (probably a storage room) and Room 17 (the governor's main living area). After 1172 the governors took up residence on the first floor of Ireby's Tower, above what is now the main entrance to the castle. The new accommodation would have been lighter, warmer, less damp and much more commodious than any of the rooms in the keep.

So, if the governor was living in Ireby's Tower when the first Carvings came to his attention, why would he have wanted the decorations to adorn a small obscure room in the keep, which he would have had no reason to visit, rather than a room adjacent to living quarters? The answer must surely be . . . that he was living in Room 17 when he asked for Room 22 to be decorated!

So who might that governor have been?

1) The first governor of Carlisle Castle was King David of Scotland, whose tenure lasted from his capture of the fortress in 1135 until his death in 1153.

2) He was followed by his twelve-year-old grandson, Malcolm IV, who was basically evicted by his distant cousin Henry II in 1157.

3) From 1157, when Henry II ruled England, until 1172, the only English governor of Carlisle Castle appears to have been Robert de Vaux or de Vallibus, Baron of Gillesland – but more of him later in Part 3, 'The Dacre Courtships, Marriages and Beasts'.

If one accepts the hypothesis of a governor ordering the decoration of Room 22 with a hunting scene, then the choice is that of two Scottish kings or a Baron of Gillesland. Personally, for no particularly good reason, my choice is King David I of Scotland.

* * * * *

The Best Kept Secrets of the Western Marches tried to make sense of the toing and froing of Cumberland between the kingdoms of England and Scotland in the 200-year period before King David gained possession of Carlisle Castle. There is no point in repeating this story, but a tad more detail about the Anglo-Norman and Scottish Royal families – along with a mention of the numerous Matildas or Mauds – might help to place in context the events outlined above.

William the Conqueror was married to Matilda of Flanders and amongst their ten children were two kings of England – William II, or William Rufus, and Henry I. One of their six daughters was also called Matilda and another, known as Adela of Normandy, married Stephen, Count of Blois. They produced a son, whom they named Stephen, who eventually became King Stephen of England.

William II, who was the second son of William I, never married and died in a hunting accident in the New Forest in AD 1100 – exactly like his elder brother Richard twenty-five years earlier. William I's third son, Henry, then became king in 1100, the same year of his marriage to the twenty-year-old Matilda of Scotland, the sister of King David I of that country. Henry I had only two legitimate heirs – a son, William Adelin, who was the Duke of Normandy, and a daughter – yet another Matilda (henceforth referred to as Matilda of England to avoid confusion). William Adelin drowned at the age of seventeen, when the 'White Ship', on which he was attempting to cross the English Channel, floundered in a storm off Barfleur in Normandy.

This left Matilda (of England) as Henry's sole legitimate heir – at a time when women did not rule medieval Western European countries. She, as it turned out, was of a different mind, having been married to Emperor Henry V of the Holy Roman Empire until his death.

At the time of her father's death in 1135, Matilda (of England) had been married to Geoffrey V Plantagenet, Count of Anjou, for seven years, but was not considered eligible as the next ruler of England. That title was given to Stephen of Blois, the son of Adela, Countess of Normandy (and daughter of William I), and Stephen, Count of Blois.

Stephen had two things to support his claim to the throne – firstly, he was, like Matilda, a grandchild of William I, but, secondly . . . and more importantly . . . he was a man. The rivalry between Stephen and Matilda sparked off nineteen years of intermittent civil war, referred to as the Anarchy, which lasted from 1135 to 1154.

One of the first consequences of this civil war was the invasion of Northern England in 1135 by King David I of Scotland, Matilda of England's uncle. His motives for heading south across the Border, capturing the castles of Alnwick, Wark, Norham, Newcastle and Carlisle, might have been threefold – support for his niece and, as well as a degree of self-interest, a degree of Anglophobia. David came to an accommodation with Stephen in the 1st Treaty of Durham and in return for a cessation of hostilities was awarded Carlisle and Northern Cumberland. The other castles were returned to Stephen.

On his arrival in Carlisle, David found the stone keep of the castle only half completed. The original construction had been ordered by Henry I, but the latter's design was not to David's liking. The high-ceilinged Great Hall on the first floor was reduced in height to accommodate the addition of another floor – a new second floor, which would contain a governor's suite of rooms – Rooms 17, 21, 22 and 23 – which David intended to occupy.

There were, as it happened, and doubtless to everyone's confusion, two other Matildas in David's family – firstly, his sister, Matilda of Scotland (Henry I's wife and Matilda of England's mother); and, secondly, his wife, Matilda, Countess of Huntingdon, who gave him a son, Henry, who inherited the titles of Earl of both Huntingdon and Northumbria. He died prematurely in 1152, one year before his father.

King David apparently spent many happy years in Carlisle and is said to have welcomed his grand-nephew, the twenty-year-old Henry Plantagenet, Matilda of England's son and future Henry II of England, on a trip up to Carlisle in 1153 with a knighthood – possibly dubbing him in Room 17.

The next year, 1154, was a year of great change due to the death of two kings. King David I died in Room 21, the oratory or chapel next to Room 17 in Carlisle Castle, and was buried in Dunfermline Abbey in Fife. In Dover, Stephen I passed away and was buried in Faversham Abbey in Kent.

England and Scotland both had new kings – the twenty-one-year-old Henry II of England and the twelve-year-old Malcolm IV of Scotland. The latter was no match for his distant cousin and, although blood was and is still thicker than water, when Henry came north he kindly asked Malcolm to vacate Carlisle Castle. In return he was given the Earldom of Huntingdon, to which his father and grandmother before him had had title.

(Clearly, the name Matilda or Maud was a very popular name for girls, especially those belonging to the nobility, around the turn of the first millennium. It may have been made so due to the Queen of East Francia or St Matilda of Ringelheim, who lived between 895 and 968 and whose grandmother, another Matilda, was Abbess of Herford Abbey in Saxony. The former was a devoutly religious woman, who was renowned for her acts of charity and the founding of many religious houses. Her feast day, 14th March, is still celebrated to this day in Saxony and Bavaria.)

The Matildas of England and Scotland.

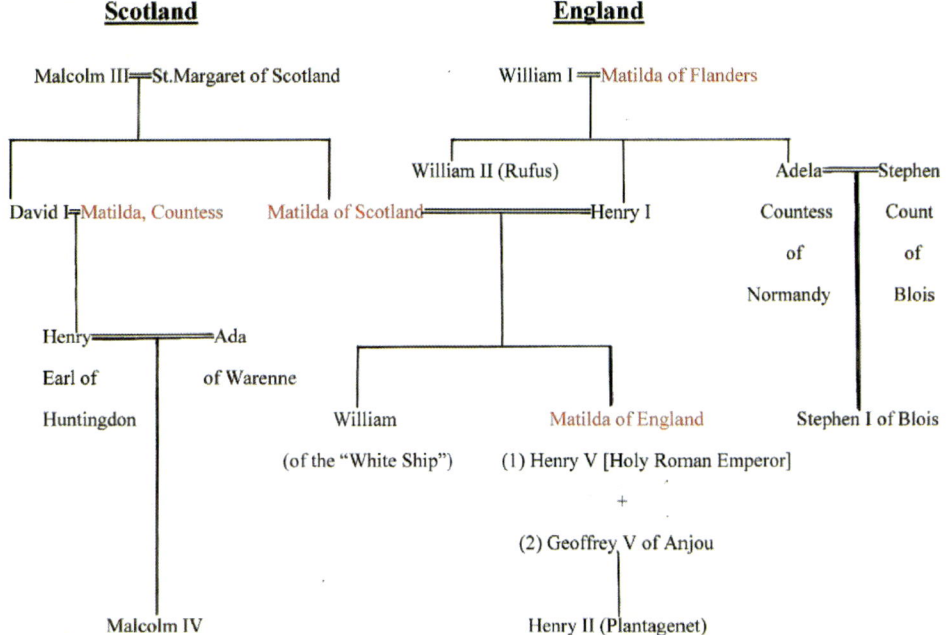

The Dacre Beasts.

PART 3 – THE DACRE COURTSHIPS, MARRIAGES AND BEASTS

In the Middle Ages for aristocratic families to survive and prosper they needed better titles, more land, increased influence, as many allies as possible and access to more money.

All of the above could be achieved through royal patronage or rewards. Initially, many started their rise in ascendency and power with a title and gift of land from William the Conqueror for services rendered during the Norman Conquest.

Similar steps enabling nobles to climb up the ladder were achieved throughout the ages by supporting the king in the numerous civil wars which occurred from time to time. Of course, the reverse could happen. Choosing the wrong side would inevitably mean, if you were captured rather than killed in battle, a one-sided treason trial – no defence allowed – and execution by beheading. (Lesser mortals and nobles low down in the pecking order were hanged, drawn and quartered.) Another consequence of being convicted of treason would be that you and your family would be attainted – your land and titles would revert to the Crown and your heirs would inherit nothing.

Civil wars were tricky businesses and the outcome usually went in favour of the monarch – but not always. A way to ensure a family's property and titles stayed within the family was to place bets either way – i.e. have family members actively supporting both sides. That way the loser would die – one way or another – and theoretically forfeit everything, but having a relative on the winning side would ensure the family lands and its titles stayed within the family. The Stanleys were particularly successful in the use of this cunning plan, but one wonders how it was decided who would support whom. Perhaps, the more senior member joined the royal camp and the more junior supported the contender for the throne.

Another aspect to treason is expressed rather philosophically in an old adage which suggests that 'Treason never prospers, for if it did, who would dare call it treason?'

* * * * *

A much less dangerous way of acquiring all of the above 'goodies' was through marriage. Arranged marriages were how such things were managed, as only peasants married for love or, more often than not, married because of a badly timed pregnancy, an angry family and a persuasive priest.

Sometimes marriages were arranged to gain support and mutual protection – an alliance through the marriage bed as it were – so that both families could survive a difficult period. Such occurrences were not unusual in a violent age, when, more often than not, might was right.

If simple advancement was the aim of the exercise, the trick was to look for and find an heiress – the sole child of a wealthy family, but not one so much higher up the social ladder than your own family as to make your proposal – made through an intermediary – be seen as totally unacceptable.

Sometimes, especially if the heiress was the ward of another family, there could be obstacles standing in the way of a fortune-hunting and impoverished suitor. Her guardian might have other plans – such as a marriage to someone within his family circle or even to himself. However, if the girl was willing, an elopement with the suitor might be arranged. The guardian would, of course, use another word to describe this romantic flight – *abduction*.

The Dacres used this form of courtship more than once. The first time was in 1315, when Ranulph Dacre removed the thirteen-year-old Margaret de Multon or Moulton from Warwick Castle, where she was a ward of King Edward II. Margaret was the sole heir of Sir Thomas de Multon, Lord of Gillesland and had been married – 'in name only' – to Robert de Clifford, when she was aged seven years. This was not an unusual practice at the time, when such preliminary unions often predated the real marriage by many years. What was unusual in this case was that her father and Ranulph's had entered into a premarital contract prior to the 'marriage' to Robert de Clifford, which was then judged legal when this arrangement was discovered.

The word *abduction* was quickly dropped and the elopement seen as all above board. Ranulph duly married Margaret on 4th February 1315 and Edward II was gracious enough to pardon Ranulph two years later, despite Ranulph, his father, William, and another brother being involved in the judicial murder of Edward II's lover, Piers Gaveston, in 1312. The result of this union was the birth of four children, William,

Block 32 – A Dacre/Neville marriage.

An Heraldic Dolphin – naiant.

An Heraldic Dolphin – haurient.

Mary, Ralph and Thomas; but – more importantly as far as Ranulph Dacre was concerned – he became Baron Dacre of Gillesland.

The second abduction was carried out by Thomas Dacre, who turned out to be the family's brightest star in the firmament. He took Elizabeth Greystoke, the Baroness of Greystoke, from Brougham Castle near Penrith, where she was in the custody of the Clifford family. This occurred around 1487 and the couple were subsequently married – bringing into the world eight children.

(As a wild guess and in consequence of these two occurrences, one might reasonably suspect that there was no love lost between the Cliffords and the Dacres.)

Thomas Dacre, as a result of this marriage, became 1st Baron Dacre of Greystoke adding that title to his own – 2nd Baron Dacre of Gillesland. He became a Knight of the Bath in 1503 and, doubtless due to his role as Captain of the Border Light Horse and Lancers (the Dacre Prickers) at Flodden Field in 1513, was awarded the title of Knight of the Garter in 1518. Thomas also acquired Morpeth Castle through his marriage to Elizabeth – and the manor of Henderskelfe, which subsequently became the site of Castle Howard.

By 1518 he was then riding high on the 'Wheel of Fortune' and wished to celebrate his success with some form of token – one which stated who he was and where the Dacres had come from. Who thought of the idea is unknown, but what came into existence around 1520 were the Dacre Beasts, which may not have been called that at the time.

Four six-foot-tall exotic animals, elaborately carved in oak and richly painted and gilded, were produced. They were in fact the heraldic supporters of the coats of arms of families which over the centuries had been important either directly or indirectly in the rise of the Dacres to their current status. The Dacre Beasts originally stood in the Great Hall of Naworth Castle from the early 1520s until 1999, when they were bought by the Victoria and Albert Museum.

An alternative explanation for their existence is that they were produced for Thomas Dacre's funeral, which took place at Lanercost Priory in 1525, presumably on the orders of his son, William Dacre. It has also been suggested that they originally stood in another Dacre family home – possibly Kirkoswald – before being taken to Naworth. In 1844 the Dacre Beasts were damaged by a fire and then faithfully restored by Anthony Salvin in 1849.

At some point in the 19th century, staves with tinned copper banners bearing the coats of arms were added to the magnificent Dacre Beasts to indicate which family they had originally been associated with as supporters.

* * * * *

Of all the families the male heirs of the Dacre family married into – and there were quite a few – only the supporters of four were chosen as designs for the Dacre Beasts. For one reason or another – and it was mostly that other unions did not benefit the Dacres sufficiently – the Garnets, Nevilles, Maxwells, Douglases, Fizhughs and Parrs were not chosen. The Nevilles, after the fall of Richard Neville, the Kingmaker, must have been personae non-gratae, but the Parrs were very important in the re-establishment of the Dacres.

(Catherine Parr, who married Henry VIII on 12th July 1543, was the great niece of Mabel Parr, who had married Humphrey Dacre, who was Thomas Dacre's father – but that, of course, was all in the future and unforeseeable when the Dacre Beasts were carved in the 1520s.)

* * * * *

So, what was the sequence of events; the relationship with lands owned and governed by which families; the appearance of the Dacre Beasts; and basically 'Who married Whom?' all those years ago.

The briefest of any family timeline is at best tortuous . . . but the following is offered as the simplest explanation possible. The who and the when are not that difficult to identify, but why a particular beast had been chosen as a heraldic supporter for any of the families involved is lost in the mists of time.

For an even more simplified and at-a-glance version, see the simple flow chart on page 75 – 'Marriages and the Dacre Beasts'.

1) The Vaux Family and the Gryphon:

The Vaux family, originally called Vallibus, came from Normandy and four brothers of that name accompanied William the Conqueror in 1066 in his cross-Channel invasion. However, it is not until much later that a connection between a member of that family and the Border country can be made. Hubert de Vaux, the son of Seigneur Robert de Vallibus de Vaux, born circa 1105 at Irthington in Cumberland, was ceded the Barony of Gillesland by King Henry II in about 1160, as a reward for expelling the Scots from this section of the frontier. Gillesland was one of three baronies created by Ranulf de Meschines, Lord of Cumberland, around 1120 – the other two being Burgh by Sands and Liddel near Kirkandrews.

Hubert de Vaux died in Gillesland in 1164 and his grandson, another

70

Hubert de Vaux and Baron of Gillesland, who had married Margaret de Burgh, had only one child in 1224 – a daughter called Maud or Matilda, who has been described as possessing the title of 'Landy of Gillesland'. Maud married Thomas II de Multon of Burgh by Sands in 1236.

* * * * *

With regard to the Gryphon, the Victoria and Albert Museum has two particular observations to make on the Internet – one misleading and the other fascinating.

The Gryphon (also spelled Griffon or Griffin) is referred to as a 'supporter of the Dacre Family of Gilsland, Cumbria', however, Tullie House, Carlisle's impressive museum, in an article printed in 2000, with the addition of a few words, clarifies the situation – 'A Supporter of the Dacres of Gilsland through Hubert de Vaux, first Baron of Gilsland and his son, Robert – who founded Lanercost Priory in 1169'.

Anyone familiar with the illustrations in Lewis Carroll's books might have a sense of déjà-vu when looking at the Gryphon in the Victoria and Albert Museum. The political cartoonist and illustrator John Tenniel produced ninety-two drawings for *Alice in Wonderland* (Macmillan, 1865) and *Through the Looking Glass and What Alice Found There* (Macmillan, 1871). Three depict a Gryphon, which the Queen of Hearts commands to escort Alice to see the Mock Turtle in order to hear his stories.

The 9th Earl of Carlisle had apparently invited Tenniel to stay at Naworth Castle (possibly around 1860), where he would undoubtedly have seen the Gryphon and all the other Dacre Beasts, which had been restored by Anthony Salvin in 1849 after the fire of 1844.

2) The Moulton Family and the Ram:
The ancestral line of the de Moulton, Moulton, de Multon or Multon family is confusing. The first reliably traceable member appears to be Lambert de Moulton, born in 1121 at Moulton in Lincolnshire.

(Before that there are references on the Internet to people like Aelfgarus de Muletune, born in 975 in Ely, who sired a son, Brictive de Moulton, seventy-five years later in 1050! This is incredible, as is the name of Muletune, which sounds like Boy's Town or Mule Town in Walt Disney's *Pinocchio*.)

After Lambert de Moulton, there appear to have been two Thomas de Multons – both born in Moulton with the first in 1146 and the second in 1174. The latter Thomas, known as Thomas, Lord of Egremont Castle, died in Burgh by Sands, the birthplace of his son, yet another Thomas, to his second wife, Ada de Moreville, in 1218. It was he who married Maud de Vaux in 1236, becoming Baron of Gillesland in the process.

Unbelievably, another three Thomases followed one after another and all were born in Gillesland. The final one, born in 1275, was Sir Thomas de Multon. His first wife was Nicole de Mauley, the daughter of Piers de Mauley le Tierce in the modern department of Loire. After her death, Thomas remarried – this time to Eleanor de Burgh, who bore him two daughters and a son. However, it was the eldest daughter, Margaret, born in 1300 at Mulgrave Castle, Whitby, who succeeded to the title of 2nd Baroness Multon of Gillesland.

It was at this point the first Dacre appeared on the scene – Ranulph Dacre, whose tale of the abduction of young thirteen-year-old Margaret has already been told.

* * * * *

The Ram, which is a really feeble-looking creature with the appearance of a hornless and shorn sheep shortly after clipping and nothing like the 'Swaledale Bullyboys' on the Cumbrian Fells, is referred to in a Victoria and Albert Museum download as 'a supporter of the Multon (or "Mouton", French for sheep and hence ram) coat of arms'.

3) The Dacre Family and the Bull:

A fairly lengthy, but inevitably catalogue-like list of the major players of the Dacre family from William Dacre, born in 1200, to the sad young George Dacre, who died in 1569, thus ending the long-running medieval 'mini-series', was laid out in *The Best Kept Secrets of the Western Marches*.

* * * * *

The Victoria and Albert Museum has two comments to make about the Bull.

Firstly, it mentions the battle cry of Thomas Dacre's 'Prickers' at Flodden Field, "A red Bull, a red Bull, a Dacre, a Dacre", which apparently put fear into the hearts of the Scots and French. Supporters of Carlisle United at Brunton Park, I'm sure, have more chilling words to say about the 'ref' than that.

Secondly, 'A Christian visitor to Naworth', who was accompanied by some ladies, was horrified at the 'Bull's gilded Pizzle' and decried the

'Decorator' – presumably Anthony Salvin – for his bad taste. On behalf of the nation, I can only but say, "Go for it, Salvin!"

4) The Greystoke Family and the Dolphin:

The first traceable Greystoke seems to have been Ligulf de Greystoke, who was born around 1030 in Greystoke, Cumberland. His name and date of birth indicate that he was definitely not a Norman, but in 1069 he was given permission to stay on as the local lord – indicating Greystoke was just south of the land governed by the Scottish King Malcolm III and inside William the Conqueror's domain. He duly built a wooden tower surrounded by a stockade, which also sounds like a standard motte-and-bailey Norman fortification. His grandson Ivo began building a stone tower, which in structure has all of the hallmarks of a Border pele tower.

By the early 1300s the castle was enlarged and castellated, but, by and large, nothing seemed to happen to the castle and its occupants, surrounded as they were by the forests in the centre of the county.

A slight hiccup occurred when the male line died out in the late 13th century. The problems really started when Thomas de Greystoke's successor, Robert, died without issue. The line then passed to his brother, William, whose only son, John, died without leaving an heir. The succession reverted back to the descendants of the female line i.e. Joan Greystoke, Thomas's daughter and John's cousin.

Joan had married William FitzRalph, Lord of Grimsthorpe, in Lincolnshire. Their son Ralph FitzWilliam became the 1st Baron FitzWilliam, but thankfully was known by a much less complex name, Ralph de Greystoke (1st Baron Greystoke of Greystoke and no relation to Tarzan, it has to be added).

And so the family went on and on through the decades without a great deal happening to them and then, on 10th July 1471, Sir Robert Greystoke and his wife Elizabeth (née Grey) produced a daughter, who was also christened Elizabeth that same day in Morpeth, Northumberland. She was the eldest granddaughter and heiress of Ralph Greystoke (5th Baron Greystoke). Her elopement from the Clifford's castle of Brougham near Penrith by Thomas Dacre around 1487 has already been told.

Something has to be said about the 'fish' – the Salmon (or is it really a mammal, a Dolphin?), which, as a supporter of the Greystoke coat of arms, is officially described as a Dolphin.

Any casual observer might suspect that the original carver was not exactly au fait with the shape and form of a dolphin, but knew what a salmon looked like – hence his resultant carving. Most people at

73

the time were equally lacking in detailed zoological knowledge, so the appearance of the 'Beast' was not questioned.

Students of heraldry will, however, be aware of the stylised appearance of Dolphins on various coats of arms – both in the horizontal or naiant and vertical or haurient forms – either in books or as seen carved on the sides of the Dacre tombs at Lanercost Priory.

Whereas it has to be said that the Dacre Beast in the Victoria and Albert Museum does resemble quite accurately that on the tombs, it does differ from both the real thing and the drawn heraldic images in one very obvious characteristic – fish scales. Perhaps the carvers didn't really know what heraldic Dolphins looked like either!

* * * * *

Block 32 on page 67 shows a Dacre scallop and a Neville ragged staff. Both are family badges and are connected by a medieval knot – in this case a Dacre knot. The trio of images indicates a marriage, which could been between:

1) William Dacre, 2nd Baron Dacre, and Katherine Neville of Raby in 1342; or
2) Thomas Dacre, 6th Baron Dacre of Gillesland, and Phillipa Neville, 3rd daughter of the 1st Earl of Westmorland, in 1406.

This symbolism might also be the origin of the phrase 'tying the knot!')

The Vaux Family
"THE GRIFFON"
↓
Harold de Vaux (1010 to ?)
↓
Hubert de Vaux (1105 to 1164)
[Granted the Barony of Gillesland in 1160]

↓

Maud de Vaux (1224 to 1293?)
Landy of Gillesland married Thomas de Multon/Moulton in 1236
Formerly 1st Baron of Egremont and becomes Baron of Gillesland.
The Moulton/Multon Family
"THE RAM"

↓

Margaret Moulton (1300 to 1361)
2nd Baroness Multon of of Gillesland married Ranulph Dacre,
who became Baron Dacre of Gillesland (1290 to 1339)
The Dacre Family

↓

Thomas Dacre 2nd Baron Dacre of Gillesland (1467 to 1525)
married Elizabeth Greystoke (1471 to 1516) in 1487,
who was the 6th Baroness Greystoke of Greystoke and whose husband
Thomas Dacre became 1st Baron Dacre of Greystoke.
"THE BULL" & "THE DOLPHIN"

The fox.

76

PART 4 – BLOCKS AND PICTOGRAMS

The discovery that a number of the sandstone blocks in Room 22 had on their surfaces purposely placed groups of images that collectively formed stories, or pictograms was a bit of a revelation. However, as the passing on of tales was a well-established Cumbrian tradition, it should not really have been a great surprise – although such confabulations owe more to Baron Munchausen than to Baron Dacre.

Equally, over a 400-year period it was bound to happen that one of the twenty or so carvers would eventually veer away from producing simple images like mermaids and try to put into pictures the words in his mind. Being illiterate that would have been his only way of passing on his stories of people and events – other than by word of mouth.

Additionally, it is also heart-warming and reassuring to discover that history isn't just a mind-numbing collection of facts and dates, transcribed from documents written on vellum in Latin or Norman French and converted into dry dissertations by academics.

* * * * *

In *The Best Kept Secrets of the Western Marches* five pictograms were only briefly explained – there being insufficient space to do them justice within its pages. The following is an attempt to give a much fuller account of what the carvers wanted to tell us about their world. Also included, is much more background information, so that the reader can put the carvers' tales into the centre of the larger account of what many call – for the lack of a better word – history.

The connection between some of these collections of images and the interpreted stories might seem in some cases . . . a little tenuous. In such cases, the error, if there is one, is in trying to find a hidden meaning where none might exist. Indeed, it is possible that some of the images are just simple Carvings of objects, animals and people without there being anything else to explain other than a simple description of what they obviously are.

As it's all a matter of opinion, there is little or no proof as to what the carvers really intended to portray. We know they were illiterate – 95%-plus of the people at the time were – but, if they had wanted to tell us a story in picture form, then this must surely be how they would have done it.

Of course, if that was what they were trying to do, then we must take into account that truth and legend might have been one and the same to them. However, we should not feel too superior, as even today the information we are bombarded with from the media isn't always 100% gospel-true . . . but then again, are the Gospels 100% accurate either?

On the other hand, if the carvers were not really trying to tell us anything and the following accounts are just anecdotal historical footnotes, then where is the harm in promoting an understanding of the past though simple tales of yesterday and its people?

* * * * *

The pictograms are presented, not in the numerical sequence of the blocks or in the order of their credibility, but as their stories would have occurred in time. All you have to do is to imagine yourself as a visitor to Room 22 – all those years ago – looking at each story block in turn, from the first to the last, and learning about your fellow man's version of what was happening around him on the Borders . . . just a few years, months, weeks or even days ago.

1) Block 31 – A Fox and Two Birds or a Tale and a Half:

Block 31 (pages 31 & 76) is situated in the middle of a row of blocks at the bottom of the South Wall. It depicts three animals – a fox and two birds. The fox is sitting in a boat or perhaps a nest and is viewed suspiciously by two feathered onlookers.

It is an intriguing image, which was first explained to me by a local Cumbrian historian around 2003 as an image relating to a Viking board game called fox and geese or as it was referred to in Old Norse . . . *halataƒl*. As it happened neither assertion was true and my attempt to authenticate both turned into a wild goose chase.

Dragon boats.

Halatafl.

Hnefatafl.

Fox and geese.

80

'Bishop' Fox preaching to a congregation of birds.

Sir Andrew de Harcla.

Halatafl or tail board is just one – and possibly the first – of a number of old board games which the Norsemen invented and played between around AD 900 and 1300. This one is played on a seven-by-seven squared board with twenty-two men on each side. It is deceptively like draughts, but cunningly different – a game based on forward and side movement, but mostly on slaughter. It also has hidden tactical depths.

The object is either to 'kill'/take all of your opponent's men (by jumping over each in turn or in sequence and landing on a vacant square, as in draughts) or to 'capture'/occupy one of his two corner squares or to force him to retreat involuntarily to either of these squares.

The next game was called *hnefatafl*, which means 'king's table' and has a variety of different forms. Each Norse settlement – Irish, Welsh, Scots et cetera – developed their own version. Boards varied in size from seven by seven squares right up to nineteen by nineteen. The greater the size of the board, the more men were involved, but the basic layout of each game was the same. The 'king' with his small group of followers occupied the centre of the board and was surrounded on four sides by his enemy's army – always twice the size of his. The object of the game was for him to reach a corner square or for his opponent to capture him. Movement, as in *halatafl*, was orthogonal rather than diagonal as in draughts, but in *hnefatafl*, as opposed to *halatafl*, the pieces moved like a rook in chess, rather than one square at a time. Also unlike *halatafl*, the pieces could move backwards. Capturing an opponent's piece was achieved by occupying the two squares on either side of it.

The final two of these Viking games were fox and geese, and fox and sheep, of which the spin-off is the modern, much simpler, fox and hounds. The first two are played on boards which developed into what became peg solitaire boards, but fox and hounds is, of course, played on a draughtboard.

The boards for these games vary slightly in size – the latter being a little larger – however, both are cruciate in shape. The basic principles of play are the same. The 'fox' must kill a certain number of 'geese' or 'sheep' by jumping over them – in any direction – and the latter must pin the 'fox' against the side of the board or in a corner. The 'sheep' version also allows a win for the ovine general if he can move a specified number of his sheep across the board to an area called the 'paddock'.

Having learnt all these games and actually played *halatafl* on a converted draughtboard, another penny finally dropped – albeit like a pebble sinking through honey – the image on the block in Room 22 had absolutely nothing to do with *halataf1* or any of the other games! The basic connection was flawed, as the birds on the block look nothing like geese. There might have been an excuse for the Greystoke Dolphin resembling in some respects a Salmon, but everyone – absolutely everyone – must have known what a goose looked like!

* * * * *

A much more plausible explanation for Block 31 can be found in the images and stories related to Reynard the Fox found in bestiaries and manuscripts and on misericords. There is a slight variation in the theme of these 13th- and 14th-century nursery stories, but basically the fox is depicted as being sly and devious. He is variously shown, thinly disguised as a friar or bishop, preaching to a group of gullible birds. His intention is plain – to lull his audience into a false sense of security and then eat as many of his congregation as possible.

Most of these graphic tales seem to indicate that he will be successful in his quest. One, however, tells of the bird's acquiescence in their fate, but with the proviso that the fox allows them to say a few prayers before their demise. The twist in the fox's tail is that the birds continue praying and praying and praying endlessly. (The drawing offered relates to a medieval French watercolour.)

Some of the other stories insinuate more subtle messages and attacks on the Church's hypocrisy and dissimulation – a preamble, perhaps, to the forthcoming Reformation. Others are just variations on the proverbial tale of the wolf in sheep's clothing.

* * * * *

F. J. Field described Block 31 in his article entitled 'The Carvings in the Entrance to Major MacIvor's Cell, Carlisle Castle', in the journal of the Cumberland and Westmorland Antiquarian and Archaeological Society in 1937 as – 'A ? Fox issuing from a ? boat between two birds, which are regarding it with manifest interest.'

If the birds are definitely not geese, as previously suggested, then what are they? The one on the right might be taken for a duck and the other might just be a nondescript common or garden small English bird, but . . . could it represent something else? Indeed, could the trio be

84

a parable-like tale – depicting the fox's well-known characteristic of slyness in the context of a contemporary event, which could only be safely portrayed in a most obtuse manner?

* * * * *

On 12th May 1316 King Edward II granted a charter to the mayor and citizens of Carlisle in thanks for their defeating Robert the Bruce's siege of the city the previous year. The initial letter in the first sentence on this document is a large illuminated medieval 'E' in and around which is a scene depicting Sir Andrew de Harcla, the Castle's governor, hurling a spear at one of the Scottish besiegers. On the governor's shield, which is basically a red cross on a white background, is a small black bird – suspiciously like the one carved on the left-hand side of Block 31.

If this is correct, Block 31 is sending out a very subtle message – one which the carver was at pains to hide from the new governor, Sir Anthony de Lucy. By placing these images in such a poorly lit and easily overlooked position, his message stood a good chance of going undetected. By choosing a less than obvious cartoon-like form for this message, he might have hoped that only those in the know would have understood what he was trying to convey.

And what might that message have been? – 'I and many others in the garrison and City of Carlisle, still support the actions of our former governor, Sir Andrew de Harcla. We deplore the deeds perpetrated by both Sir Anthony de Lucy and our dishonourable and sly king, Edward II, both of whom we hold responsible for the cruel death of Sir Andrew by hanging, drawing and quartering in Harraby on 2nd March 1323.'

These are powerful words indeed and require an explanation.

* * * * *

Andrew de Harcla was born at Hartley Castle near Kirkby Stephen in Westmorland circa 1270 to Sir Michael Harclay, Sheriff of Cumberland, and his wife, Joan FitzJohn. In 1303 he was knighted by Thomas of Lancaster, a man who was not only the first cousin of King Edward II, but a noble who would play an even greater role in de Harcla's fortunes some years later. By 1311, Sir Andrew became sheriff of the county and then, in 1315, as commander of the Carlisle garrison, he held at bay Robert the Bruce, who was besieging the city.

The pinnacle of his career came in 1322, when he trapped, defeated and captured his previous benefactor, Thomas of Lancaster, at the Battle of Boroughbridge near Harrogate. Edward II was overjoyed on hearing the news, as for ten years he had been waiting patiently to wreak bloody vengeance on the man he blamed for the death of his lover, Piers Gaveston, outside Warwick in 1312.

Sir Andrew was awarded the titles of 1st Earl of Carlisle and of Lord Warden of the English Marches. This gave him almost plenipotentiary powers in dealing with the Scots and their king, Robert I, who had soundly thrashed Edward II at the Battle of Bannockburn on 24th June 1314. However, there was a catch to wielding these powers – a time limit of twelve months, during which he could take independent action without seeking the approval of Edward II.

Whether by accident or purpose he overstepped the mark and the time limit. Exasperated by the King's inability or possible negligence in trying to put an end to the almost twice-yearly massive Scottish *chevauches* deep into the north-east and north-west of England, he decided to act. He had the support of the other nobles, but nevertheless he acted alone on this occasion – crossing the Border on 3rd January 1323 with only a small military escort he headed for Lochmaben.

There he made a peace treaty with Robert the Bruce. The raids would cease with the proviso that Robert would be recognised as the independent king of the autonomous Kingdom of Scotland. De Harcla asked Robert the Bruce not to make public this agreement, as he would have to personally persuade Edward II of the merits of such a treaty . . . at the appropriate time.

That time never came about, as someone talked and talked and talked to Edward about what de Harcla had allegedly agreed to with Edward's bitterest of enemies. In addition to signing a peace treaty, de Harcla was said to have agreed to the following:

1) Should Edward II not agree to the treaty, then Robert the Bruce and de Harcla would ensure by military means his acquiescence.

2) A certain Sir James Douglas, one of Robert's trusted lieutenants, would in due course pay de Harcla substantial amounts of money for his help in arranging the treaty.

3) The hand of one of Robert the Bruce's daughters was also promised to de Harcla in return for his services to Scotland and to Robert I.

On hearing this information only one word must have slipped from King Edward's mouth – *treason.*

De Harcla was summoned to appear before his king to give an account of these allegations. However, shortly after this order was issued another shortly followed – for the arrest of de Harcla. This was to be carried out by Sir Anthony de Lucy, an old enemy of de Harcla and mayhap the man who had informed Edward II about the meeting at Lochmaben Castle.

Accompanied by Sir Hugh Lowther, Sir Richard Denton and Sir Hugh de Moriceby, Sir Anthony headed post-haste to Carlisle. They entered the castle on 25th February without any difficulty, suggesting that de Harcla, who was no fool, was unaware of the original summons and therefore unprepared for what was about to happen. The unarmed earl was found in the keep occupied with paperwork and duly arrested. Only one man apparently resisted the arrest – the Keeper of the Inner Gate – and he was slain by Sir Richard Denton. Sir Andrew submitted to his fate and ordered the rest of the garrison not to intervene.

Things then occurred with breakneck speed. Sir Geoffrey le Scrope, the King's justiciary, arrived on 2nd March and with undue haste de Harcla was arraigned, tried and found guilty of treason on the 3rd. That same day he was executed at Gallows Hill, a mile south of the city gates. After being degraded as a knight, he suffered the 'traitor's death' – that of being hanged, drawn and quartered – but not before saying a few final words: "You have disposed of my body at your pleasure, but my soul I give to God."

(He might easily have voiced what Thomas Wentworth, 1st Earl of Strafford, would say of his king, Charles I, 300 years later – Psalm 146: "Put not your trust in princes!")

So perished one of the Borders' mightiest of heroes. His quartered body was sent for display to York, Newcastle and Shrewsbury – the fourth part went ironically to the place he had so valiantly defended in 1315 – to Carlisle Castle. His head was apparently placed on a spike on the Rickergate in Carlisle, but later may have been dispatched to London.

De Harcla was never pardoned, despite Edward II's coming to a similar agreement with Robert the Bruce six months after the execution and ardent pleas from the family. Five years later his sister, Sarah, managed to get hold of what was left of his body and give it a Christian burial in 'The Cathedral of the Dales', St Stephen's Church, Kirkby Stephen.

* * * * *

The beneficiaries of this sad story were undoubtedly the common people in the north, who were now finally able to get back to living a normal life free of massive and repeated Scottish raids.

The people of Carlisle and its garrison had lost their leader and protector, but life went on – with a new man in charge of the castle . . . who was none other than Sir Anthony de Lucy, who held the post for the next seven years – three years longer than the life of his benefactor Edward II, who died a particularly unpleasant and unnatural death in Berkeley Castle, near Bristol, on 27th September 1327.

* * * * *

And did the story end there? I personally think not, as men like Sir Andrew de Harcla are never truly forgotten. And sometimes a more permanent reminder of their existence is left for all to see – like . . . possibly . . . the Carving on Block 31.

It's still there with Edward II in the centre depicted as a fox; Sir Andrew is on the left and that 'duck egg' – de Lucy – on the right, who clearly never knew of the existence of this epitaph to a 'Border hero' . . . otherwise he would have defaced or erased it.

Two Templar knights on a road outside Jerusalem.

The Outremer.

2) Block 33 – Good Sir James or the Black Douglas:

There is a soldier on Block 33 (page 31) on the South Wall of Room 22 – on the extreme right-hand side just under the top row of blocks. On both his right and his left is a heart and they were what inspired the search for the explanation of exactly what he was doing there.

Indeed, if you look closely, another heart can be seen directly on top of his helmet. It looks slightly different in shape to the other two and appears somewhat out of place. A wider search reveals another two more – one on Block 11, just below the unfinished crucified man on Block 10 on the right-hand side of the doorway to Room 23 and another on Panel 41 on the back of the door.

These two do not seem to be associated with any other images and their significance is unknown, but those on Block 33, close as they are to the soldier, seem associated with him. Hearts then as now, and indeed for centuries before him, were a sign of love, but in his day similar emblems were usually worn as battlefield badges or symbols on coats of arms. However, hearts were not commonly employed as such.

An initial search revealed that only one family had a heart as part of its coat of arms and then only after 1330 – the Douglas family from the south-west of Scotland. Subsequent enquiry has revealed more information, which will come to light as the story of the first two hearts unfolds.

The carving of such a figure, possibly one Scottish in nationality, by a peasant on the English side of the Border, alongside such a unique heraldic device, which came into existence on a specific date, surely means something very significant – a story and one well known on either side of the Border. If the date was around 1300, which seems likely from his armour, and if his surname really was Douglas, then the soldier must be Sir James Douglas – otherwise known as Good Sir James or the Black Douglas – depending on whether you were Scottish or English.

* * * * *

The story of Sir James Douglas is fairly well known, but not in its entirety. He was a formidable soldier, as well as being a friend and trusted lieutenant of King Robert the Bruce of Scotland. It is said of him

91

that he made a promise to his dying friend, which led not only to his own death, but to the adoption of a heart on his family's coat of arms. However, there is much more to it than that and the full story is well worth the telling.

It all started on 10th February 1306, when Robert the Bruce had a less than pleasant rendezvous with an old enemy, John III Comyn, Lord of Badenoch and of Lochaber – nicknamed for good measure the Red Comyn. They met in the chapel of Greyfriars Monastery in Dumfries in front of the high altar – on holy ground and therefore on neutral territory. This should have ensured the safety of both, who were apparently in the process of discussing the future kingship of Scotland, which both had a strong interest in. A fracas broke out and John Comyn was either killed instantly by Robert the Bruce or possibly severely wounded – to be, shortly afterwards, finished off by the latter's men.

For this wanton act of desecration, King Edward I of England petitioned Pope Clement V to excommunicate Robert the Bruce, who by 25th March that year had been crowned king by Bishop William Lamberton at Scone near Perth. Robert countered the Pope's anathema by asking his friend, Robert Wishart, the Bishop of Glasgow, for absolution, which, of course, he granted.

Final absolution and the lifting of the papal interdict from Scotland by Pope John XXII did not occur for another twenty-two years. In the meantime King Robert had made a promise to God to atone for his heinous sin by going on Crusade – an act which Urban II, who initiated the 1st Crusade in 1096, had promised would lead to the absolution of all sins, including any future ones, even those committed while on crusade.

Robert never fulfilled his promise to God, being too busy with his almost continuous warfare with the 'auld enemy', the English, and, despite Pope John's pronouncement, the murder of the Red Comyn and his subsequent failure to carry though his oath weighed heavily on his soul. Then, on his deathbed at Cardross Manor in early June 1329, with his trusted friends around him, Robert the Bruce asked if anyone would help to lift this burden from his troubled soul.

What he actually wanted to happen is uncertain, but the possibilities are as follows. That after his death, his embalmed heart:
1) Would be taken on Crusade to the Holy Land.
2) Would be taken on Crusade to another destination.
3) Would be placed on the altar of the Church of the Holy Sepulchre in Jerusalem.

The end result of any of the above would have been, in Robert the Bruce's eyes, an act worthy of Pope Urban II's promise of absolution.

Sir James Douglas agreed to carry out his friend's final wishes, but so apparently did six other Scottish knights:

a) Sir William and Sir John St Clair of Rosslyn.
b) Sir Robert and Sir Walter Logan of Restalrig.
c) William Keith of Galston in Ayrshire.
c) Symon Locard of Lee, who would hold a special place in the group as the trusted holder of the key of the silver casket which contained Robert the Bruce's heart.

It is also been suggested that four others might also have made up the 'band of brothers' who left with Sir James Douglas on his sacred quest:

a) Sir Kenneth Moir.
b) William Borthwick.
c) Sir Alan Cathcart.
d) Sir Robert de Glen.

* * * * *

After Robert's demise on 7th June 1329, his heart was duly removed, embalmed and placed in a conical silver casket, ten inches in length. It was attached to a heavy-duty silver chain, which Sir James hung around his neck.

In the spring of 1330 the group of knights set sail from Montrose and made landfall at Sluys in Flanders, where they remained for the next twelve days, possibly because of inclement weather and/or unfavourable winds. It was there that they learnt of the 'Reconquista' – King Alphonso XI of Castile and Leon's war to expel the Moors from Southern Spain, which sounded to them very much like what Urban II would have considered a Crusade.

(King Louis IX of France had been involved in two crusades outside the Holy Land – the 7th Crusade to Egypt (1248–54), when he was captured by the Mamelukes and the 8th Crusade to Tunis (1267), where he died of dysentery.

Indeed, there had even been one in Southern France between 1209 and 1229, which had been on the instigation of Pope Innocent III and was fought against the Cathars, whom he considered to be heretics.)

In Sluys the seven Scottish knights had ample time to consider the situation and the Holy Land seemed totally out of the question, as:

1) Jerusalem had been in the hands of the Seljuk Turks, since its capitulation to Salah ad-Din Yusef ibn-Ayyub – otherwise known as Saladin – on 2nd October 1187.
2) The last Christian toehold in the Outremer – the Christian kingdoms in the Holy Land – the city of Acre, had fallen after a six-week siege as recently as 18th May 1291.

The decision they made was not that difficult in the end, and so with a new impetus for their quest they headed off to Spain. On their arrival in Seville, they were greeted warmly by King Alphonso, who invited them to join what was in effect an international brigade with Sir James becoming its commander. The Scots first saw action at the siege of Teba, twenty-five miles north-west of Malaga, which necessity dictated had to be broken off on the impending arrival of a large relief force led by the Moorish King of Granada, Muhammad IV. After regrouping, the combined Christian army attacked and the Battle of Teba commenced in August 1330.

As ever with the accounts of many medieval battles, there is a great deal of confusion as to what actually happened, but two things do not appear to be in dispute:

1) William Keith was not present on the battlefield due to a broken arm.
2) Sir James Douglas and all the other Scots, apart from Symon Locard of Lee, were killed at Teba.

At some point during the confused sprawling battle, Sir James and his contingent became separated from the main Spanish army due to a cunning Moorish stratagem – a feigned cavalry retreat. Then, trying to rally his men, Sir James is reported to have taken the silver casket containing Robert the Bruce's heart from around his neck, and whirled it in a circular motion above his head before hurling it into the thick of the enemy. Charging forward, he addressed not only his companions, but his dead friend with the following words, which have echoed down through history, "Now pass thou onward before us, as thou were wont, and I will follow thee or die!"

The above account first saw the light of day in a poem called 'The

94

Brus', which was penned by John Barbour in the 16th century and seems to have caught the last moments of a brave Scottish knight in all his vigour and elan.

What actually occurred was, perhaps, no less dramatic. Sir James, at the point of extracting himself and his men from the trap they had fallen into, noticed Sir William St Clair in dire trouble. Without any fear for their own safety, he turned his steed around and led the other Scotsmen back into the melee to rescue their brother in arms. It was all in vain, as they died to a man.

Indeed, only two of the seven who had set out from Scotland lived to tell the tale – William Keith, who had not taken part in the battle, and Symon Locard, who had been involved in his own struggle with the Moors in another part of the battlefield.

After the battle the bodies of Sir James and the other four knights were found along with the silver casket, but whether it was still around Sir James's neck or not depends on which version of his legend you want to believe. King Muhammad was so impressed by the selfless valour of these infidels that he returned every one of their bodies, including that of Sir James plus the silver casket, to King Alphonso.

Of course, in those days these were no such things as body bags, refrigeration or total-body embalmment – the latter having been lost in the sands of Egypt centuries earlier. The surviving two Scottish knights set about initiating the grisly work of preparing the bodies of their friends for repatriation to Scotland – in the customary method of the time.

It seems unlikely that they personally performed the dismemberment of the bodies and the boiling down of the bones, but one account does mention that these two removed and embalmed each one of their friends' hearts – and that the heart of Sir James was placed in another silver casket. Whatever else remained of their friends, other than the bones, which had been dried and placed in containers, was given a Christian burial. Keith and Locard then returned home to Scotland with their precious cargo.

The bones and heart of Sir James Douglas were buried in St Bride's Chapel in Lanarkshire and, as a result of the fulfilment of his promise to Robert the Bruce, the Douglas family was granted a red heart on their coat of arms in perpetuity.

Bruce's heart was interred in front of the altar of Melrose Abbey and not in Dunfermline with the rest of his body. The casket was rediscovered in 1921 and subsequently reburied in a new lead container beneath the floor of the chapter house of Melrose Abbey. In 1996 the container and casket were exhumed and subjected to fibre-optic analysis, before finally being laid to rest once more at Melrose on 22nd June 1998. They are still there beneath a commemorative plaque unveiled by Donald Dewar, Secretary of State for Scotland, on 24th June 1998.

* * * * *

But the story does not end there, as the actions of Symon Locard of Lee, the 'Key Holder to the Bruce's Silver Casket', initiated the final chapter of an already gripping tale.

At the Battle of Teba in another part of the battlefield he apparently captured a Moorish emir, whose mother paid Locard a ransom for his release in the form of a medallion. It sounds almost like a fairy tale, as the medallion had special healing powers – the ability both to reduce fevers and to stop bleeding. It was given a name – the Lee Penny – which subsequently became the basis of a novel written by Sir Walter Scott called *The Talisman*.

It is said that Symon Locard not only changed his name to Simon Lockhart, but also added a heart and a fetterlock to his family coat of arms to commemorate his role as the keyholder . . . and as a final touch the following words were added as a family motto, '*Corda serrata pando*' – 'I open locked hearts.'

* * * * *

(Perhaps, the third heart on Block 31 is genuine after all – the one on the soldier's helmet being that of Robert the Bruce and the other two being those on the Douglas and Lockhart shields. It is an attractive thought, but unlikely, as the carver would almost certainly have been unaware of the Lockhart story.

The Internet also indicates that the Logan and Keith family coats of arms also bear a heart, but there appears to be some dispute about the validity of including this heraldic device on their shield. However, if two of the five families of the seven knights who escorted Robert the Bruce's heart on Crusade have been allowed to include a heart in their coat of arms, it seems somewhat churlish for the others not to be so allowed – unless, of course, there is some serious doubt as to whether they actually accompanied Sir James Douglas to Spain.)

The Douglas coat of arms.

The Lockhart coat of arms.

97

St Sebastian and the Great Pestilence.

3) Block 4 and the First Martyrdom of St Sebastian:

Two figures in their birthday suits have stared out at the world with blank enigmatic faces and dead lifeless eyes for 650 years. They can be seen on Block 4 (page 101) on the North Wall to the left of the doorway to Room 23. Both are surrounded by religious figures and icons. One, the smaller of the two, is definitely up to no good and has been sensibly ignored. The other, studded with projectiles, has puzzled some experts for years and most do not know what to make of her . . . or is it him?
The printed views of ten historians are set out below:

1) 'No. 55 – A naked female figure front-faced with a circular head-dress, hands on hips, and with three large arrows piercing each side of the body' in 'The Carvings in the Entrance to Major MacIvor's Cell, Carlisle Castle' – by F. J. Field – Article II of the journal of the Cumberland and Westmorland Antiquarian and Archaeological Society (1937) – read at Penrith on 7th July 1936.
2) 'St Sebastian' in *Carlisle Castle, Cumberland* by G. P. H. Watson and Geoffrey Bradley – published by His Majesty's Stationery Office (1938); reprinted for the Ancient Monuments & Historic Buildings, Ministry of Works, 1951.
3) 'St Sebastian' in *Carlisle Castle* by G. P. H. Watson and Geoffrey Bradley an official guide published by the Ministry of Public Building and Works (1937); 11th impression, for Her Majesty's Stationary Office, 1970.
4) 'A woman pierced by six large arrows' in *Carlisle Castle: A Survey and Documentary History* by M. R. McCarthy, H. R. T. Summerson and R. G. Annis – with contributions from D. R. Perriam and B. Young – published for English Heritage by the Historic Buildings & Monuments Commission for England (1990).
5) No mention in *Carlisle Castle* by Colin Platt and Mike McCarthy – published by English Heritage (1992); 6th reprint, 2004.
6) 'Carving of a naked woman attacked with spears' in *Carlisle Castle* by Henry Summerson – an English Heritage guidebook published by English Heritage (2008); 2nd reprint, 2013.
7) 'Elaborate late medieval graffiti showing the martyrdom of St Edmund, Carlisle Castle, Cumbria' in *Medieval Graffiti: The Lost*

Voices of England's Churches by Matthew Champion – published by Ebury Press (2015).

With regard to the easier of the two problems, I think it is generally accepted that missiles with feathered flights on their non-pointy ends are without a doubt . . . arrows!

As to whether the naked figure is that of a man or a woman might be more problematical. Indeed, the female shape, and in particular her bottom, was just that for the Italian Renaissance's most accomplished artist, Michelangelo di Lodovico Buonarroti Simoni. He frequently placed spade-shaped female buttocks on men and heart-shaped male buttocks on women – spades and hearts as in two of the suits on playing cards. This confusion has been blamed on Michelangelo's lifestyle, but no one really knows.

With regard to the preferred shape of the female form in the latter part of the Middle Ages, we are told that it verged towards overt voluptuousness, whereas previously the flatter-chested shape was deemed to be the ideal.

Of course, in portraying the naked form, we should not expect our carvers to have the same knowledge of anatomy as can be gleaned from either Gray's or Lockhart's anatomy books. However, they would have been more than capable of distinguishing and portraying the naked shapes of an adult man and woman.

The so-called naked woman on Block 4 is definitely android in the upper body, unlike the figure of the Madonna and Child in Block 5 (below and to the right and probably also carved by the same person) – which is clearly female in form. However, the lower body of the 'woman' – to put it bluntly – has been drastically and very crudely altered to make it appear to resemble that of a woman.

Such disfigurements have occurred in the best of organisations. The most well known happened in the middle of the 16th century during the Council of Trent or Trento in Northern Italy – the Roman Catholic Church's Counter-Reformation council. Not only did the council fail to address satisfactorily the very real problems within the Church, which had caused Martin Luther and others to break away from Rome, it produced an edict which was to cause havoc in the Vatican.

The edict proclaimed it was inappropriate to display in any religious building representations of the naked male or female buttocks, breasts and genitals – whether in paintings, on frescoes or on statues. This resulted in someone surreptitiously going round the Vatican with a

Block 4.

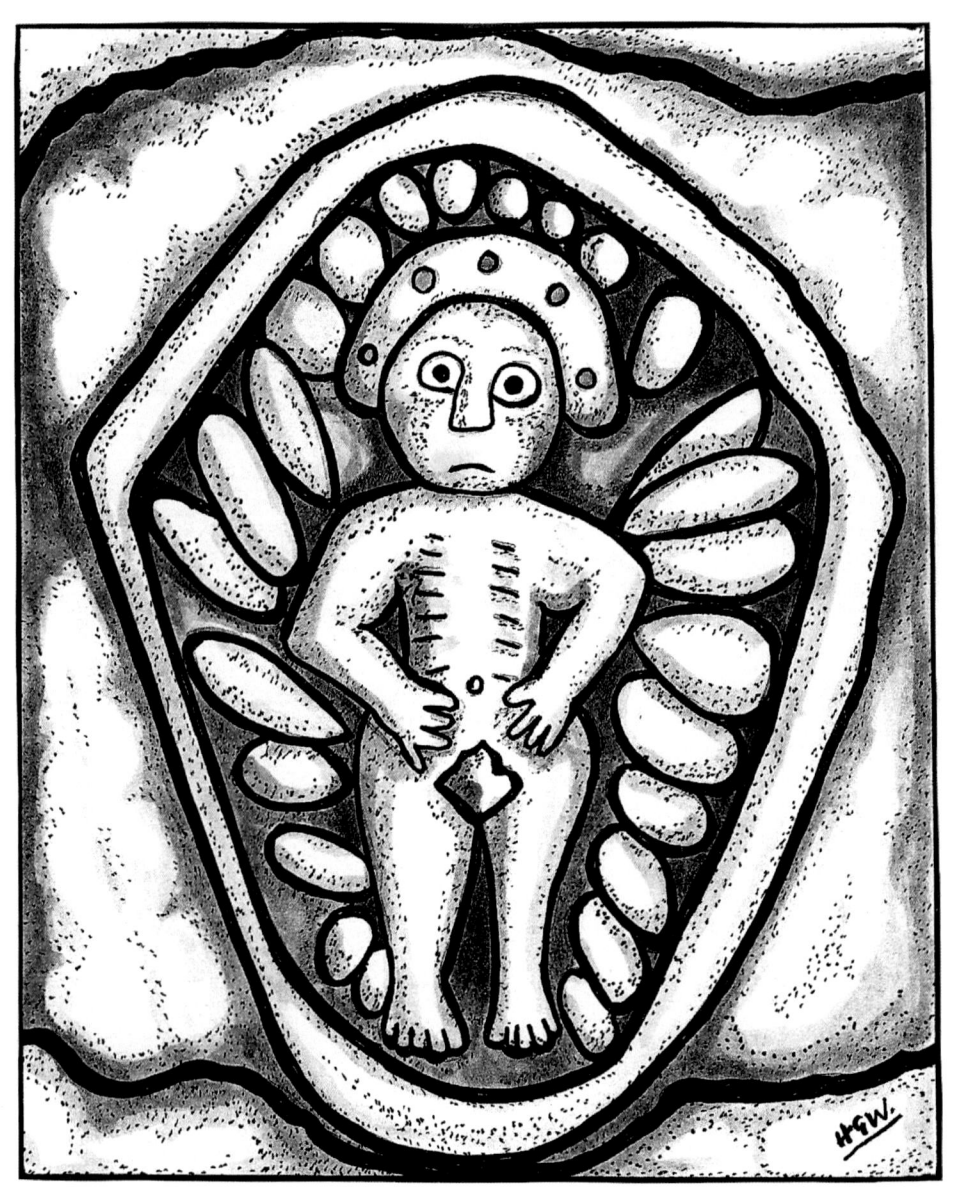

Block 32.

hammer and chisel removing male parts from statues – willy-nilly, as it were!

A sequence of events then ensued:

1) The resultant damage so upset Pius IV that in 1557 he arranged for the production of plaster fig leaves to cover the crudely damaged parts of the male statues.
2) Then between 1644 and 1655 Innocent X came up with a more permanent solution – metal fig leaves.
3) Between 1758 and 1769 Clement XIII, on learning that the original saboteur had missed a few appendages, made certain that they were adequately covered.
4) However, not to be outdone by his predecessors, Pius IX in 1857, having discovered Clement XIII's cover-up, personally went round the Vatican with a hammer, striking off every one of the remaining parts.
5) Finally, Pius's successor, Leo XIII, did the decent thing and between 1878 and 1903 ensured that Pius's zealous behaviour was hidden in the time-honoured fashion – with more fig leaves.

Now, no one is suggesting that the papacy has had anything to do with Room 22 – other than the beatification of the, as yet, nameless figure portrayed on Block 4. However, the same sort of activity as described above has clearly occurred in Room 22, but for different reasons.

There are three small naked male figures on the walls of Room 22 – one next to the 'woman' and two others on the South Wall on Blocks 30 and 32 (page 102). All appear to have been carved by the same person and each one is graphically accurate, as is the activity they appear to be performing and enjoying. However, certainly one – if not two – of these naked male figures on the South Wall are missing a part of their anatomy – as if a victim of Pius IX's hammer. Vandalism is exactly what it was, as these two carvings are too far apart from each other for the damage to be accidental. The emasculation clearly occurred after the original carving was completed, as the roughened surface where the part was darker than the rest of the stone on each figure.

The small naked man next to the 'woman' is intact, but might not have remained so for long if the vandal had continued with his work – and fallen victim to the change which the 'woman' on Block 4 has undoubtedly endured.

* * * * *

Quickly moving on to a less basic problem, it is time to identify the male figure. Surrounded, as he is – with the exception of his unsavoury companion – by a number of religious figures and sacred images, it seems likely that he is a saint and, from the arrows piercing his body, is in the process of being martyred.

It seems unlikely that our carver way up in Carlisle – separated by 200 miles and 500 years from East Anglia – would have known anything about St Edmund, who may have been killed in this manner.

The story of the martyrdom of the King of East Anglia on 20th November 869 is steeped in legend. He was captured after a battle against the Danes, who banded together in a force known as the Great Heathen Army, which rampaged up and down England between 865 and 878. After his capture, St Edmund is said to have been martyred with arrows shot by no lesser a Dane than Ivar the Boneless, the son of Ragnar 'Hairy Breeches' Lodbrok. Edmund was then decapitated and his head thrown into a wood, where it was later found by his followers – guarded by a wolf.

If the above story of St Edmund's martyrdom is anywhere near the truth, then some might say he got off relatively lightly at the hands of Ivar the Boneless – unlike King Aella of Northumbria two years earlier. He is said to have caused the death of Ragnar Lodbrok by having him thrown into a pit full of poisonous snakes. In revenge for his father's death, Ivar ensured Aella had the worst of all deaths – the blood eagle. While still alive and tied to a frame, the back of his chest was opened up either side of the spine and then a number of ribs were cut away, so that his lungs could be pulled out to form flapping 'wings' covered in blood.

The last major band of the Great Heathen Army was led by Guthrum, who was defeated by Alfred the Great at the Battle of Edington in 878.

As for other saints who were martyred by a firing squad of archers, there only appears to have been one other – St Sebastian. Who he was and why his image and those of the other saints and symbols around him ended up on the North Wall of Room 22 of Carlisle Castle in the latter part of the Middle Ages is a matter of both religious tradition and conjecture.

Sebastian is said to have been born the son of a wealthy Roman in Narbona (modern-day Narbonne in Southern France). He apparently joined the Roman army during the reign of Emperor Carinus around

AD 282 and – just like St George – became an officer in the Praetorian Guard of the Emperor Diocletian in Rome.

The latter was in many ways a stern and conservative man, following the pagan beliefs of his time and pursuing – with vigour – a relentless persecution of Christians. Hundreds died in the process, including at least a dozen named saints. Sebastian, who had converted to Christianity, was to be one of these.

He was sentenced in AD 288 to be a living target for a group of Mauritanian archers, who left him for dead tied to a tree – so riddled with arrows that he resembled a sea urchin. St Irene of Rome found him barely alive and nursed him back to health. Incensed by Diocletian's treatment of Rome's Christians, Sebastian subsequently waited for and accosted the Emperor as he passed through the Imperial Forum. The end result was predictable – Diocletian dispatched a few of his bully boys to find Sebastian and give him a second and final martyrdom.

He died either from clubbing or stoning and might easily have disappeared into history as a mere footnote – another little-known saint and victim of Diocletian in the fourth year of his reign – had not someone decided to dedicate an altar to him in the Church of St Peter in Pavia in the 7th century, during the reign of King Gumburt.

At the time, a devastating pestilence was raging across the land, but the building of this altar seemed to cause a halt to its progress. Thus, the name St Sebastian became associated with averting pestilences and his story subsequently appeared, along with that of other saints and church dignitaries in the *Legenda Aura* or *Golden Book* in the year 1260 or thereabouts. From then on, if you wanted protection form an ongoing pestilence, it was to St Sebastian that you prayed.

Nearly 100 years later, possibly in the depths of Kyrgyzstan in Central Asia, a new scourge of God – the Great Pestilence – appeared out of nowhere and swept across the world killing millions. It was caused by a bacterium called *Pasteurella pestis* (now renamed *Yersinia pestis*) and was transferred from person to person by fleas carried on black rats.

The pestilence was characterised by the rapid appearance of a fever and black boils or buboes in the groin, neck and armpits – hence the name Bubonic Plague. It later changed into an inhaled and a more readily communicated form – the Pneumonic Plague. The incubation period for both was between one and six days and death usually followed within thirty-six to forty-eight hours.

A children's nursery rhyme, thought to have originated in 1881, vividly illustrates the rapid and fatal nature of the pneumonic form, which was also prevalent in the Great Plague of London in 1665:

Ring a ring o' roses,
A pocket full of posies,
A-tishoo! A-tishoo!
We all fall down.

It is said of the 14th-century pestilence, now commonly referred to as the Black Death, that it arrived from the continent in 1348 on a boat, docking at either Bristol or Weymouth – two places which have since been unfairly referred to as towns which one should avoid like the plague. Within a year it had spread to Wales and Ireland, as well as travelling up north as far as the Anglo-Scottish border.

It did not appear in Scotland until 1350, after an army, wishing to avenge the defeat of King David II at Neville's Cross in 1346, invaded Northumberland and Durham. The Scottish commander had heard the north-east of England was somewhat depleted in defenders due to an unknown sickness and unwisely took advantage of the situation. Along with the cattle, slaves and other booty, the hapless Scots took home with them a cartload of *Pasteurella pestis*.

The Black Death had a mortality rate of around 33% and revisited the British Isles five times between 1348 and 1393, killing an estimated 2,000,000 people out of a population of around 6,000,000.

Treatment was non-existent, but suggestions, as to what should be done to prevent catching the Great Pestilence were mind-numbingly pathetic:

1) The continuous ringing of church bells and the firing of primitive cannons were thought to rid the air of the miasma or 'night air', which was supposed to be the cause of the disease.
2) People were urged not to wash; to refrain from eating meat and not to exercise.
3) Cats and dogs were killed, as they were thought in some way to spread the illness.
4) Penance and self-flagellation were encouraged, until vast numbers of self-whipping crowds became a public nuisance.

As to what you should do if you actually caught the disease, two pieces of advice were offered:

106

1) Rub a chicken against the black boils and the problem will be transferred to the chicken.
2) Stay at home . . . and presumably die there alone.

The Church offered solace and advice in the form of comfort and intercession between God and members of their congregations – for what was allegedly God's punishment meted out to a sinful world. However, as the priests were also dying off like flies, few of the Church's representatives were at hand to administer any form of assistance to their flocks.

The only hope anyone had was that their own natural immune system might afford them protection against the infection – but, of course, none of this was known at the time.

Today, even with the news of the recent outbreak of the Ebola virus in West Africa, we can have no real comprehension of the terror which stalked the land in the 14th century hand in hand with the Black Death.

There was nowhere to hide and little help from anywhere, as whole villages and communities disappeared, as wave after wave of death crossed and recrossed the country again and again. The 'Wheel of Fortune' spun out of control and cast hundreds upon hundreds into hastily dug plague pits. The world was rapidly being depopulated and perhaps coming to an end.

Without the intercession of priests, the terrified peasants sought protection either from St Sebastian or prayed directly to God. Perhaps, the religious images around and including that of St Sebastian himself on the North Wall of Room 22 were in effect 'prayers in stone' – carved on top of earlier images, which had now no meaning to the desperate carver, who sought protection from this mindless scourge, which was devouring all around him.

Perhaps, the half-finished upper torso of a crucified Christ on the right-hand side of the doorway to Room 23 was such a prayer – unfinished, because Death tapped the carver on the shoulder before his entreaty could be answered.

Luck, the Lancastrians and the 'Wheel of Fortune'.

4) Block 26 – The Battle of Towton, Palm Sunday, 29th March 1461:

Block 26 (page 111) with its deceptively simple images can so easily be overlooked, surrounded, as it is, high up on the left-hand side of the South Wall, by so many outstanding carvings like those of Lord Thomas Dacre at Flodden and a number of Dacre Beasts – Vaux Gryphons and Greystoke Dolphins. Equally, it might easily be mistaken for a block like Block 32 (page 102), which shows the badges of the Dacre and Neville families connected by a marriage knot – in this case a Dacre knot.

This block does not depict a marriage. It is something entirely different – a commemorative plaque carved in honour of senior members of the Dacre, Percy and Roos families, who fought together in Henry VI's Lancastrian army on Palm Sunday, 29th March 1461, at the 'Bloody Battle of Towton'. Such a small block, yet behind it is the story of the biggest battle ever fought on British soil, where approximately 10,000 men died in a swirling snowstorm – about half as many as paid the 'butcher's bill' on the first day of the Battle of the Somme on 1st July 1916.

And who exactly were the men these badges – three scallops, three fusils and a water bouget – represent? We can name specifically seven of them, but there were many more who died in the ranks of their lord on that terrible day, ending up without a mention in large anonymous grave pits.

1) Randolf Dacre, 9th Baron Dacre of Gillesland.
2) Humphrey Dacre, Randolf's brother.
3) Henry Percy, 3rd Earl of Northumberland.
4) Richard Percy, Henry Percy's brother.
5) Sir Ralph Percy, another of Henry Percy's brothers.
6) Thomas Roos or de Ros, 10th Baron Roos of Hamlake.
7) Henry Roos, probably Thomas Roos's brother.

* * * * *

Each has his own tale to tell, but the story behind Block 26 – the role Carlisle played in the Cousins' War and the Battle of Towton – does not begin or end in the snows twelve miles south-west of York in March 1461. It began nearly a year before at the Battle of Northampton – on

10th July 1460 – just five years after the onset of that thirty-two-year conflict.

By that time, in the so-called Wars of the Roses, the balance of power between the two rival factions was about even. The Lancastrians were led, albeit nominally, by the intermittently insane King Henry VI, and the Yorkists were commanded by another member of the House of Plantagenet, Richard, Duke of York – hence the name by which the conflict might better be called – the Cousins' War.

Then, the worst of all circumstances for the Lancastrian cause occurred . . . once again King Henry, who had been captured by the Yorkists after the 1st Battle of St Albans on 25th May 1455, lost another battle and fell again into the hands of his enemies near Northampton.

This time, he wasn't automatically freed by the victors in the hope they would be pardoned for their taking up arms – not against him, of course, but against his treacherous councillors, the Earls of Somerset and Northumberland. No, this time the issue of who would rule the country would be sorted out once and for all – for now and for the future. There would be no return to business as usual by the mad king and his incompetent advisors.

Henry VI was taken to London, where in October of that year Parliament agreed to most of the Duke of York's wishes – the latter having just returned from Ireland, where he had ruled as Lieutenant. The anointed king, Henry VI, would be allowed to remain on the throne, wielding minimal powers, but on his death he would be succeeded by the Duke of York and thereafter his heirs. The young Prince of Wales, Edward of Westminster, was thus disinherited and there was absolutely nothing Henry could do but accept the situation.

The Lancastrians were now in great disarray – with Henry Beaufort, Duke of Somerset, trying to reorganise what forces he had at his disposal and with Margaret of Anjou, Henry VI's French queen, and their young son, Edward of Westminster and Prince of Wales, scuttling off up north in the hope of obtaining money, men and arms from the Scots.

The King of Scotland, James III, was just a boy of nine summers, who had succeeded his father, James II, on 3rd August 1460, when a Flemish cannon called 'The Lion' had exploded near the thirty-year-old Scottish monarch during the siege of Roxburgh Castle. James II's wife, Mary of Guelders, then became the Queen Regent of Scotland and it was with her that Margaret of Anjou had to strike a bargain.

Block 26.

111

Winter vespers in Yorkshire.

For ten days around New Year of 1461 at Lincluden Abbey, near Dumfries, the two argued and haggled over what should or could happen. On the face of it, the contest – for that is exactly what it was – seemed fairly evenly matched. Two women faced each other and tried to come to terms over the future of their children – for that is what it was all about to them. Both were foreign queens – one from the Low Countries and the other from France – one a widow and the other a fugitive, separated from her captive husband. Both, however, shared a common and unyielding determination – forced on them by the hard school of life – to abandon the pose of a behind-the-scenes heir-producing queen – to become a ruler and powerbroker in their own right.

The power struggle continued into the New Year with neither woman giving an inch. It was a complete deadlock. Mary of Guelders wanted more than what Margaret of Anjou would or could offer. A betrothal between either of Mary's daughter's – the seven-year-old Mary or the five-year-old Margaret – to the seven-year-old Edward of Westminster was fine, but that marriage could only take place in the distant future. Mary of Guelders wanted something concrete and she wanted it then and there in 1461 – not years in the future! It is believed she really wanted the city of Berwick, but that was not something an English queen, especially one born in France, could give away without losing whatever little goodwill she had with her subjects.

And then the stalemate was broken by astounding news of a battle near Wakefield. The 'Wheel of Fortune' had turned in Margaret of Anjou's favour and a deal was quickly struck on 5th January 1461. Margaret got what she wanted, but Mary had to be content with a betrothal – between Margaret Stewart and Edward Plantagenet.

And the news . . . amazingly, was that Richard Plantagenet, Duke of York, and his son, Edmund, Earl of Rutland, had been captured after a one-sided battle near Wakefield on 30th December 1460. Both had been killed by one means or another and their heads were now on display on spikes over Micklegate Bar in York – Richard's wearing a paper crown. Alongside these two Lancastrian trophies was a third head – that of Richard Neville, 5th Earl of Salisbury and the father of Richard, 16th Earl of Warwick – the Kingmaker and right-hand man of Edward Plantagenet, Earl of March (the eldest son of the recently deceased Duke of York and the future king Edward IV of England).

Margaret of Anjou now had an army, but she had to use it and use it soon to strike a decisive blow against Warwick and the Earl of March. The former was thirty-two, but the latter only seventeen and not as yet with a reputation as a seasoned warrior and leader of men – a mantle he would shortly attain.

Margaret had to act soon, but haste was to be her undoing. She left Scotland in the middle of January 1461 with a large mixed force . . . but without the provisions she had so bitterly negotiated for. Once over the Border, Margaret's army began to swell with supporters loyal to the absent Henry VI. However, as the army grew in size, so the means to support it diminished. By 20th January, when it had reached York, living off the land had become the order of the day. As it headed south towards London, the rampaging and pillaging force was outstripped in speed by a wave of justifiable rumours of theft, slaughter, rapine, wholesale damage and wanton pillage.

Naturally, Warwick's agents took full advantage of this God-sent propaganda, but his army was not quite so competent. It collided with Margaret's much larger force at St Albans on 2nd February, when Warwick barely escaped with his life.

Fortune again favoured the French queen, whose poor, gentle, simple husband, Henry VI, was discovered sitting under a tree after the battle was over. It was now full speed for London, but it was all in vain. Unforeseen damage had crippled the Lancastrian cause. The news of what had happened to cities and towns which had opened their gates to Margaret's uncontrollable army of Scotsman and northerners had done its work. The Londoners staunchly refused to open the gates of their capital.

By 23rd February, while negotiations over access to the capital and its provisions were still ongoing, news of the assembling Yorkist contingents – the Duke of Norfolk in East Anglia; Richard, Duke of Warwick, in the Midlands; William, Lord Fauconberg (Warwick's uncle), in London; and Edward, Earl of March, in the South-West – reached the ears of King Henry and, more importantly, of Queen Margaret.

With only a few days' grace before contact with the enemy, the Lancastrian force, still desperate for provisions, began to melt away. Some of the Scots had already headed home loaded with their English booty.

Margaret, who was clearly in charge of operations, despite Henry's return, decided there was no alternative but to abandon her original plans of a campaign in the south and retreat north to the Lancastrians' natural powerbase around York. There she could regroup, reorganise and re-provision her forces, and, more importantly, recruit more men to replace the deserters.

Edward, Earl of March, must have read her mind, as, although he had fewer men, he knew he could not allow Margaret time to create an even bigger army than the one she already possessed. He headed north too – and with equal speed. What happened next, on Palm Sunday, 29th March 1461, was the Battle of Towton, just twelve miles south-west of York. Twenty-five thousand Lancastrians in an east-to-west battle line faced both the Yorkist army of 20,000 and a strong, ice-cold, snow-laden southerly wind.

The exact disposition of Henry's army, commanded by Henry Beaufort, Duke of Somerset, is not clear. He probably commanded the centre with the Earl of Northumberland, Henry Percy, on his right, in charge of the western flank of the Lancastrian army along with the Dacres and Rooses.

King Henry and his wife, Margaret, along with their son, Edward, did not attend the battle. They were at the time safely tucked away in York – well fed, rested and cosily warm in suitably royal accommodation.

Meanwhile to the south-west, the icily-cold strong southerly wind favoured the Yorkist archers, whose arrows outranged their opponents', who, in turn, because of the snow could not see where their missiles were falling. As a result of the carnage caused not only by the Yorkists' own arrows, but also by the Lancastrians' own returned missiles, Somerset felt impelled to leave his strong position above the Towton Dale and advance towards the enemy. Urging the whole Lancastrian army into the teeth of the blinding white-out, he and Henry's army crashed into the revenge-seeking forces of Edward Plantagenet and Richard Neville.

Initially, the greater Lancastrian numbers began to tell, but then in the early afternoon the ailing John de Mowbray, 3rd Duke of Norfolk, with his force of East Anglians arrived – delivering a decisive blow to Somerset's left (east) flank. Soon the Lancastrian force as a whole began to give way, crumble and then rout in a north-westward direction over the swollen River Cock. Names like the Bloody Meadow and descriptions of heaps of bodies under pink-stained snowdrifts on either side of the river, which ran red and soon became choked with the Lancastrian dead, hint at the carnage which followed.

But what of the 'Towton 7' – the leading members of the Percy, Roos and Dacre families? What happened to them? Immediately for some, and ultimately for most of the rest, nothing good was to ensue.

Richard Percy died on the battlefield, but his brother Henry, the 3rd Earl of Northumberland, survived for a time what was, in effect, a mortal injury. Carried to York in a critical state, he died the following day of his wounds. Sir Ralph Percy, the governor of Bamburgh Castle, escaped and lived to fight another day – dying in 1464 at the Battle of Hedgeley Moor, near Wooler, in Northumberland.

The brothers Roos, Thomas and Henry, fared better. Thomas, the 9th Baron de Ros of Hamlake, escaped to join the royal couple in York later that evening. At some point – possibly late in the summer of 1461 – he escaped to the continent on a ship from Berwick, returning in 1464. He also fought at Hedgeley Moor on 25th April that same year, but his luck finally ran out at the Battle of Hexham on 15th May, where he was captured. Two days later he was beheaded at Newcastle.

Sir Henry Roos of West Grinstead also escaped from Towton and was eventually pardoned by Edward IV in 1472 – becoming a sheriff and Justice of the Peace, before finally dying at the ripe old age of sixty-nine.

Of the Dacres, the elder brother, Randolf, 9th Baron Dacre of Gillesland has the more interesting – but much, much shorter – story. He died at Towton under a 'burr tree', which remained in existence until the 19th century – not like the 'Danger Tree', which can still be seen in no-man's-land on the battlefield of Beaumont Hamel, where the Newfoundlanders fought so bravely on 1st July 1916 on the first day of the Somme offensive.

Even on such a bitterly cold day, it was hot work fighting in armour and at some point in the battle Randolf Dacre dropped out of the fighting on the western end of the Lancastrian line for a rest and a drink. Taking off his helmet, he joined Harold II in dying of a not entirely unique injury – an arrow in the eye.

After the battle he was taken to Saxton, ten miles south of the carnage, and buried in the churchyard, probably with the help of members of the local Salley and Hungate families. Legend has it that he was interred in full armour still astride his horse.

The truth is less exciting, but somewhat tortuous in the telling. A tomb still stands in the churchyard of All Saints Church at Saxton and on it is an inscription – 'Here lies Ralph Lord of Dacre and Gilsland, a true soldier valiant in the service of Henry VI, who died on Palm Sunday, 29th March 1461, on whose soul God have mercy'. The tomb allegedly dates from the 17th century and may have been erected by the Moulton family, which was related to the Dacres, whose direct line had by then died out.

But what of the horse . . . and of the rest of the story? In 1749, gravediggers, taking advantage of the tomb, which seemed all but abandoned, decided to bury a Mr Gascoigne in it. On opening up one of the stone panels, they apparently discovered the erect skeleton of Lord Dacre. A little later, in 1861, other enterprising diggers, making a hole too close to the Dacre tomb unearthed the skull and spine of a horse, which appeared to project out from beneath Lord Dacre's last resting place. The skull, but not its jawbone, now apparently rests in peace in the British Museum, which is more than can be said for the whole story, which probably originated at the bottom of a gravedigger's tankard in the Greyhound Inn in Saxton.

Humphrey Dacre fled from Towton and joined King Henry, his wife and son in York – whose immediate fate will be told shortly. Humphrey was attainted that year and the family estates of the Dacres went for a time to the Fiennes – the 'Dacres of the South'. However, with the help of the Parrs of Kendal – staunch Yorkists, as it happened – Humphrey's attainder was reversed in 1473, seven years after his marriage to Mabel Parr, the sister of William Parr, 1st Baron Parr of Kendal.

(The connection between the Parrs and Dacres, who stood on opposite sides of the political divide in the Wars of the Roses, seems to have begun in earnest in 1457, when Sir Thomas Parr, Mabel Parr's father, had served on a commission to determine the heir of Thomas, Lord Dacre and 6th Baron. The decision of the committee was in favour of Randolf Dacre – the Dacre buried in Saxton's churchyard and Humphrey's brother. It is just possible that a friendship grew up between the sons and daughters of Thomas Parr, who died in November 1461, and the two boys of Thomas Dacre – Randolf and Humphrey. If so, the ties of friendship must have been stronger than political allegiances.)

Under the influence of the Parrs, Humphrey Dacre became a supporter of Edward IV and prospered. He died on 30th May 1485 still apparently a supporter of Edward's brother, Richard III. His son, Thomas Dacre, on the other hand, fought against Richard in Henry Tudor's army at Bosworth Field on 22nd August the same year.

* * * * *

Meanwhile, back in York, on the evening of Sunday 29th March 1461, the royal couple, Henry VI and his wife, Margaret of Anjou, were oblivious of the outcome of the battle in the swirling snows to the south-west. That all changed with the arrival of some bedraggled and bloodstained fugitives, who apprised the dumbfounded couple of the disastrous news from Towton.

There was no time to lose with the pursuing Yorkists hard on the heels of the remnants of Henry's routed army. The King, Queen and Prince of Wales hurriedly headed north at midnight for Newcastle. The next day they were in Alnwick, where they sought permission from Mary of Guelders to seek sanctuary in Scotland, which was, in due course, granted. The fugitives were initially housed in Linlithgow Palace – twelve miles west of Edinburgh – and then in a Dominican house in Edinburgh itself.

Although still king, Henry VI did not sit at the negotiating table in Edinburgh facing Mary of Guelders in early April 1461. Margaret of Anjou did and she knew she was in an infinitely worse negotiating position than she had been three months earlier. She wanted the same things as before – men, arms and money – but this time she knew a future marriage between her son and Mary's daughter would not be enough.

Mary of Guelders was adamant. She wanted two fortress cities – the keys to the Eastern and Western English Marches – Berwick and Carlisle. She had already received peace overtures from the young but, as yet, uncrowned Edward IV. It was even rumoured that an offer of marriage might be in the offing between the eighteen-year-old king and the twenty-seven-year-old widow.

Without much ado, King Henry IV rubber-stamped the deal and Berwick was ceded immediately to the Scots on 25th April. However, there was a problem with regard to Carlisle . . . it was not Margaret's to give, as it was now firmly in the hands of King Edward IV.

As a royal Border fortress in the middle of the civil war, it had a chequered history in terms of who controlled it. Prior to March of 1460, it had been in the hands of the Nevilles and for a brief period of time had been garrisoned by supporters of Henry VI. However, shortly after Towton on 29th March 1461, it had been re-garrisoned with Yorkist soldiers.

Lancastrian plans, forged out of necessity, were set in motion – a two-pronged attack on either side of the Pennines.

Margaret with Henry Beaufort, Duke of Somerset, and Henry Holland, Duke of Exeter, along with Henry Roos and Humphrey Dacre set out for Carlisle with a force of Scots. Lord Thomas Roos, Sir Humphrey Neville of Brancepeth (one of the few Nevilles who espoused the Lancastrian cause) and King Henry VI headed into County Durham to attack Brancepeth, near Durham City, in late June – hoping to initiate an uprising and a revival of King Henry's fortunes.

The latter did not happen and the attack on Carlisle in mid-June turned out to be more like a short-lived raid of the city's suburbs, rather than the siege which it has been called. It would appear that the Scots and Lancastrians broke into the city and caused a great deal of damage. However, the situation was retrieved by the action of the garrison and its commander, Sir Richard Salkeld, a Neville retainer from Corby, Cumberland. They managed to hold out until a relief force led by John Neville (Lord Montague, the brother of Warwick the Kingmaker) arrived on the scene within a few days. The besiegers were soon chased off with a death toll, it is alleged, of 6,000 Scots, which seems a highly suspect number.

Margaret of Anjou slipped back over the Border to Scotland along with Somerset and Exeter. Sir Henry Roos was apparently captured in Cockermouth and Humphrey Dacre may well have slipped away south to his friends, the Parrs of Kendal. In the east Henry VI, Lord Thomas Roos and Humphrey Neville also fled north to Scotland.

And that was that – the helter-skelter campaigns of 1460–61 ended with King Edward IV firmly on the English throne and the Lancastrian cause all, but not quite, in a terminal state of decline.

And so for the moment the fortunes of war between the cousins must be paused and, as what followed next is not relevant in terms of Carlisle and its Carvings, we must abandon this story between the Yorkists and Lancastrians.

However, the date when the three family badges could have been carved by a Lancastrian supporter is very relevant, but almost impossible to determine. There are only two possibilities:

1) Firstly, in early April 1461, when the news of the Battle of Towton on 29th March had just been broken to the Lancastrian garrison, but before it had been replaced by Edward IV's men.

2) Secondly, ten years later, between early October 1470 – when Richard of Gloucester, the Lord Warden of the English Marches and garrison commander of Carlisle Castle had left the city, escaping capture by Warwick the Kingmaker, who had changed sides, having espoused Henry VI's cause – and the Battle of Tewkesbury on 4th May 1471, when Edward, Prince of Wales, was killed, only hours before the murder of his father, Henry VI, in the Tower of London.

The latter date seems unlikely – there being many more important fish to fry than the remembrance of a battle and those who fought in it ten years earlier. Thus, those few days in early April 1461 seem the most likely window.

The red sandstone blocks would have been tolerably easy to carve such a simple pictogram and a couple of hours may have been all the time that was needed . . . but what a story that block holds secret!

Durham Cathedral's rose window.

121

Naworth Castle and the Armstrong Tree.

5) Block 22 – Thomas Dacre and the Dacre Prickers

If there were any doubts in anyone's mind as to whether any of the blocks in Room 22 are pictograms, there should be none whatever with regard to Block 22 (page 125). Even the most sceptical of historians should not balk at this example. They may, however, have some quibbles over the interpretation of its images and offer some alternative explanations.

Block 22 has in fact two surfaces – one is on the South Wall in the penultimate upper row on the extreme left-hand side of that wall and the other is on the upper right-hand side of the corridor leading to Room 21. Both surfaces should be regarded as comprising one single large pictogram, showing:

1) A knight wearing a sallet-style helmet and wielding a long sword in his right hand – as such he is a high-status individual in an aggressive and warlike pose.
2) To his right are two scallop badges – indicating he is a member of the Dacre family.
3) Between the scallops is a diagonal cross, a saltire or cross of St Andrew – suggesting the Scots are involved in conflict with the knight.
4) A Bull on the corridor side of the block, wearing a collar, is without doubt a Dacre Bull – one of the four Dacre Beasts – and the supporter of one specific member of that family.

Putting it all together, we have a story in pictorial form of Thomas Dacre, 1st Baron Dacre of Greystoke and 2nd Baron Dacre of Gillesland, fighting the Scots at the Battle of Flodden Field on 9th September 1513. He was then captain of the Border Light Horse and Lancers or Dacre Prickers and under the overall command of Thomas Howard, 2nd Duke of Norfolk, who defeated the invading Scots, whose king, James IV, was killed in the process.

King Henry VIII was at the time swanning about in Northern France. His English army was part of a larger force commanded by his ally, Maximillian I, Emperor of the Holy Roman Empire, who was then engaged in a war with the French king, Louis XII. Henry had left his wife, Catherine of Aragon, at home to look after the shop in his absence – little thinking that James IV of Scotland would take advantage of the situation and invade the North of England.

Henry was playing at war – the real 'noble sport of kings' – and has gone down in history as taking part in the Battle of the Spurs near the town of Therouanne in Artois, where a contingent of French cavalry was chased off the field of battle. Henry's heroic role in this minor action was to look on from the safety of the Emperor's camp.

Although he probably would not have admitted it, the Battle of the Spurs was a romp in the park compared to Flodden Field. However, to give him his due, he handsomely rewarded Thomas Dacre for his action at Flodden with the Order of the Garter in 1518, which went very nicely with his other gong of 1503, the Order of the Bath.

* * * * *

Having so described Block 22 in such detail, might an alternative explanation for the assembled images be possible? The answer is in the affirmative on two counts:

1) Firstly, could the diagonal cross represent some other heraldic device? A number of noble families had a diagonal cross on their coats of arms and the best known of these in the North of England was the Neville family of Raby in County Durham. Their shield had a white (or argent) diagonal cross on a red (or gules) background.

2) Secondly, what is the stumpy branched wooden image to the lower right of the knight? It is without a doubt the ragged-staff badge of the Neville family. When combined with a bear, we have the badge of Richard Neville, 16th Earl of Warwick – the Kingmaker of the Wars of the Roses fame.

The most prominent member of the Neville family, who had played an important role in the north-west of the country, was Richard Neville, the Kingmaker – as Warden of the Western Marches between 1446 and 1469. His younger brother John Neville, Lord Montague, had been no slouch either and had commanded a relief force, which had chased off Margaret of Anjou's mixed Lancastrian and Scottish force, which had been besieging Carlisle in June 1461. Neither of the Neville brothers had really played as important a role in the Western Marches as many of the Dacres had, so it seems likely the figure on Block 22 is not a Neville, but a Dacre.

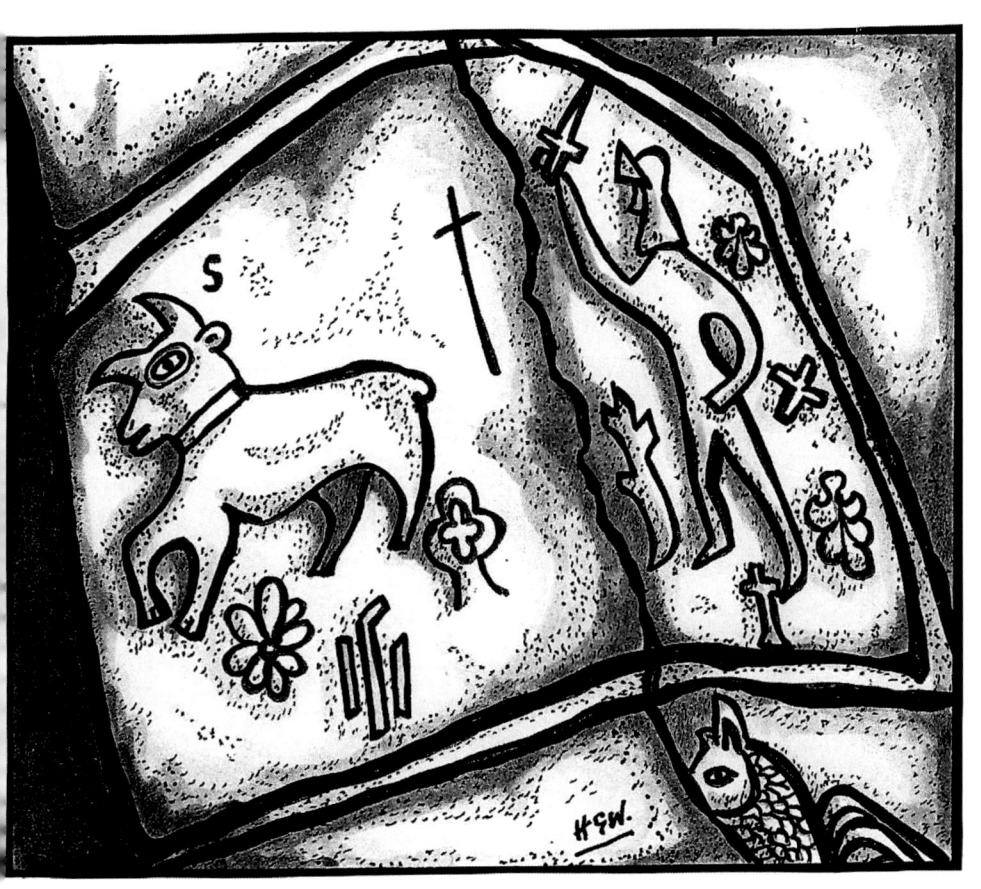

Block 22.

The coat of arms of the Dacre family.

So, is there another connection with the Nevilles? There are two and both involve marriages. Two Dacre grooms had taken Neville brides between 1340 and 1410:

1) William Dacre, 2nd Baron Dacre, married Katherine Neville of Raby in 1342.
2) Thomas Dacre, 6th Baron Dacre of Gillesland, married Phillipa Neville, the 3rd daughter of the 1st Earl of Westmorland, in 1406.

Of these two, only William Dacre seems to have been in the wars. He had fought alongside his in-law, Lord Ralph Neville – the 3rd Baron Neville of Raby – at the Battle of Neville's Cross, just south-west of Durham City, on 17th October 1346, when not only were the Scots soundly beaten, but their king, David II, was captured.

So, could the diagonal cross be an heraldic device related to the Nevilles rather than a saltire? Indeed could the knight be William Dacre in 1346 rather than Thomas Dacre in 1513?

However attractive this proposition might be, it is unlikely for two reasons:

1) Firstly, in 1346, the helmet worn by a the knight would have been a bascinet – either a sharply pointed European pig-faced bascinet or one of the rounded 'great fighting bascinets' – rather than a sallet helmet, which the figure on Block 22 is clearly wearing.
2) Secondly, the Dacre Bull was apparently not created and adopted by the Dacres – and Thomas Dacre in particular – until around 1506, nearly 150 years after the Battle of Neville's Cross.

* * * * *

In conclusion, the figure on Block 22 is, after all, Thomas Dacre at Flodden Field, but the presence of the ragged staff on that block is still a mystery. It could quite simply have been placed there in error.

More beasts and things most strange.

PART 5 – THE FINAL THROW OF THE DICE

All of the loose ends associated with the Carvings in Carlisle Castle had been neatly tied up and Room 22 had been revisited – albeit virtually, so that was that!

Then, three Internet images arrived . . . sent by Mark Douglas, English Heritage's Job Property Curator Team Leader (North) in York. They were followed by a package of photographs from my nephews in Carlisle. Both contained images of Carvings I had not seen before.

The first was referred to as the 'dove' (page 131), which looked like a fat pigeon and could, I was informed, be located on the wall beneath the Captain's Tower – opposite the Carvings of the three crudely carved fleurs-de-lis and the unexplained '1321'. It was on a block surrounded by a few initials – a large 'IW' in a mixed 'Roman and rustic' script and 'RF' looked suspiciously like the runic letters for R and A. The latter seemed to suggest that someone with a little knowledge of Old Norse script was trying to hoodwink the unwary observer. Underneath the 'dove', was a horse, which looked medieval, and below that were eight arrowheads.

The other carvings can be found in the Great Hall on the first floor of the keep – a room I had not visited for all of fifty years. Then, its walls had been completely obscured by large wooden-and-glass cases containing the uniforms and other memorabilia of the Border Regiment.

* * * * *

The first photograph revealed an enigmatic bearded face under a conical helmet (page 132). It looked almost Norse, but at a pinch might just be an unflattering caricature of the legendary Scottish reiver Kinmont Willy Armstrong (page 133), who had been the only prisoner to escape from Carlisle Castle.

He had been captured in 1596 on a 'truce day' and Walter Scott of Buccleuch, 'the Bauld Buccleuch', on whose land this had occurred, protested to the English warden about this most 'unsportsman-like' behaviour. Thomas Scrope, 10th Baron Scrope of Bolton, was not in the least impressed, being well aware of the hundreds of Scottish sportsmen who raided across the English border on a fairly regular basis, and so continued to keep Willy as an involuntary guest in Carlisle. Buccleuch responded with a daring raid, which almost went horribly wrong, due to the rescuers bringing along an undersized scaling ladder. Willy finally made his escape, much to the annoyance of Elizabeth I, who, it is said, thought this would never have happened had he been caught near Naworth Castle, where the infamous Armstrong Tree was located.

* * * * *

The second photograph appeared to be more straightforward and showed two blocks with Carvings on them (page 134). The larger one revealed a collection of initials, an arrow and three shields. The 'REW' and 'RB' were randomly placed, as was an elaborately scrolled 'H' with an arrow pointing downward through its horizontal bar. Another set of initials – 'TBB' – had been carved on a shield, which also bore the date '1603'.

Below and to the right was a smaller shield bearing two circles – one above the other. To the right of these shields was a much larger one on which were three wheat sheaves – two above and one below.

On the block above were two sets of initials – 'REW' and a 'CB' (not shown) and a large arrowhead.

Identification of the shield with the two roundlets or bezants drew a complete blank, but coats of arms bearing three wheat sheaves revealed a total of three families:

1) The Segraves were a Leicestershire family of which the first mentioned was Stephen de Segrave (1171–1241), who became Constable of the Tower of London and Justiciar of England during the reign of Henry III. Two others, both called Gilbert, became Bishops of London. The Segrave coat of arms consisted of three white/argent wheat sheaves on a black/noir field.

2) The Hattons appear to have been associated with Hatton in Cheshire, but may well have been Anglo-Norman in origin. The most notable was Sir Christopher Hatton, K.G. (1540–91), who had been born in Nottinghamshire. He became not only a Chancellor of England but also a favourite of Elizabeth I. His coat of arms had been three gold/ or wheat sheaves – two above and one below a golden chevron – all on a blue/azure field.

Another carving on the wall beneath the Captain's Tower.

An unknown bearded man.

Kinmont Willy Armstrong.

'1603' and the three wheat sheaves.

134

3) The third reference seemed very unpromising – a 'Sire Johan Comyn', whose name sounded most decidedly continental. After repeated searches on the Internet, only two names seemed to be associated with the good Sire Johan – John Comyn II and his son, John Comyn III.

And then the penny dropped – these were the Lords of Badenoch and Lochaber in Scotland. The first had been nicknamed, the Black Comyn, and the second, the Red Comyn, whom Robert the Bruce had murdered in front of the high altar in the Chapel of the Greyfriars in Dumfries in 1306.

Their family coat of arms consisted of three gold/or wheat sheaves on either a red/gules or blue/azure field and both seemed extremely promising as candidates for a family whose shield was on the wall in the Great Hall in Carlisle Castle.

As it turned out, it was the father, the Black Comyn, who was the connection, not just with the castle but also with Robert the Bruce's father, Robert, 6th Lord of Annandale, who, as it happened, had been buried in Holmcultram Abbey in Abbeytown, just fifteen miles south-west of Carlisle. This, however, did not deter his son from causing great damage to the abbey in 1319 on one of his massive raids.

Long before that, however, in 1295 Robert de Brus, senior – Robert the Bruce's father – had been made Constable of Carlisle Castle and on 26th March 1296 had successfully fended off an attack by none other than the Black Comyn and his men. Thus, there was clearly a connection between the Comyns and Carlisle Castle, but was the carving of the wheat sheaves contemporary with these events?

As it happened, the Bruces were also associated with Carlisle Castle, somewhat tenuously – i.e. through marriage. Robert the Bruce's grandfather, Robert, 5th Lord of Annandale, had married twice – the second time to Christina de Ireby, whose father's name, William de Ireby, is said to be associated with the new main gate to the castle – Ireby's Tower. The latter was built in 1167 and William de Ireby lived from 1191 to 1283, but what the connection is between the two is not known.

But where did the year 1603 fit in with all of these Carvings, which looked in style more like early 17th century than medieval? Unlike 1321, the year carved below the Captain's Tower, which was a year of non-events, 1603 was somewhat momentous. Old Queen Bess had died that year and the son of her first cousin once removed (i.e. Mary Queen of Scots) was James VI of Scotland, who became James I of England on 24th March 1603.

As he headed south towards London, multiple raids by mosstroopers or reivers broke out all along the Border. These raids into England were so devastating that the seven days of their duration became known as 'Ill Week'. The one in the west was led by Hutcheon Graham, whose 300 brigands had cut a swathe of destruction to the east of Carlisle all the way down to Penrith.

James I had reached Berwick-upon-Tweed on 6th April and was livid on hearing of these border incursions by his fellow Scotsmen. This was no way to start his reign in England. Pragmatic as ever, he appointed two no-nonsense Lord Wardens – one Scottish and the other English. The latter was George Clifford, 3rd Earl of Cumberland, who also became governor of Carlisle Castle.

King James also dispatched Sir William Selby, Governor of Berwick, west with a strong force and the situation was quickly resolved. Some of the reivers were hanged, but many like Hutcheon Graham, along with most of the Grahams were deported to the Low Countries. It wasn't long before they all sneaked back!

That is what happened in 1603, but who was 'TBB' – the initials below the date. Perhaps he was one of Selby's men, who had come over to restore order in the west or even a retainer of George Clifford. We may never know, but it looks likely that all of the carvings in the Great Hall first saw the dim light of day in the spring of 1603 in the room probably allocated as the living quarters for the new garrison.

* * * * *

And now, mayhap, the final throw of the dice has finally come to pass and all of the Carvings of Carlisle Castle have been discovered and discussed . . . that is until a few more come to light!

The end of some other tales.

The writers.

BIBLIOGRAPHY

'The Carvings in the Entrance to Major MacIvor's Cell, Carlisle Castle' by F. J. Field – Journal of the Cumberland and Westmorland Antiquarian and Archaeological Society (Article II) – 1937.

Carlisle Castle, Cumberland – Ancient Monuments and Historic Buildings and Works – Description by G. P. H. Watson and History by Geoffrey Bradley – His Majesty's Stationary Office – 1938 (reprinted, 1951).

Carlisle Castle – official guide – description by G. P. H. Watson and history by Geoffrey Bradley – for the Ministry of Public Building and Works (1937) – 11th Impression for Her Majesty's Stationary Office (1970).

Carlisle Castle: A Survey and Documentary History by M. R. McCarthy, H. R. T. Summerson and R. G. Annis with contributions by D. R. Perriam and B. Young – published for English Heritage by the Historic Buildings and Monuments Commission for England – 1990.

Carlisle Castle by Colin Platt and Mike McCarthy – English Heritage – 1992 (7th reprint, 2005).

Carlisle Castle – an English Heritage guidebook by Henry Summerson – English Heritage – 2008 (2nd Reprint, 2013).

The Secrets of Rosslyn by Roddy Martine – Birlinn Limited – 2006.

Fatal Colours: The Battle of Towton, 1461 by George Goodwin – Phoenix Non-Fiction – 2011.

Towton: The Bloodiest Battle – New revised edition by A. W. Boardman – The History Press – 2009.

Towton 1461: England's Bloodiest Battle by Christopher Gravett – Osprey Publishing – 2008.

Flodden 1513: Scotland's Greatest Defeat by John Sadler – Osprey Publishing – 2008.

Henry VI by Bertram Wolffe – Yale University Press – 2001.

Margaret of Anjou by Jacob Abbott – Forgotten Books by Amazon. Co. UK – 2015 (originally printed by Harper and Brothers, 1861).

Margaret of Anjou: Queenship and Power in Late Medieval England by Helen E. Maurer – Boydell Press (Boydell & Brewer Ltd) – 2003.

Medieval Graffiti: The Lost Voices of England's Churches by Matthew Champion – Ebury Press – 2015.

The Steel Bonnets by George MacDonald Fraser – Pan Books – 1971.

The History and Antiquities of Carlisle: With an Account of the Castles, Gentlemen's Seats, and Antiquities, in the Vicinity; and Biographical Memoirs of Eminent Men Connected with the Locality – Samuel Jefferson and by Whitaker & Co., London – 1838 (reprinted, 1923).

De Ireby's Tower in Carlisle Castle by R. Gilyard-Beer – Ancient Monuments and Their Interpretation – 1977.

INDEX

bones, 95, 117

Border Light Horse and Lancers. 69, 72, 123

Border pele tower, 73

Bradley, Geoffrey, 99

brochures on Carlisle Castle, 99

Bruce family: Robert, 6th Lord of Annandale (father of Robert the Bruce), 135; Robert I, the Bruce – see *Kings of Scotland*

Carlisle Castle: Captain's Tower, 35, 129; Dacre Postern Gate, 35–6; Great Hall, 62, 129, 135, 136; Ireby's Tower, 35, 60; Lady's Walk, 35; Room 17 – 60, 62; Room 21 – 28, 62, 123; Room 22 – 91, 103, 104, 107, 123, 129; Room 23 – 20, 27, 60, 91, 99, 107

Carlisle's charter, 85

carved images: arrow(head)(s), 17, 27, 28, 39, 55, 129; bone, 35; deer, 13, 17, 20, 27, 28, 35, 36, 39, 56; doe(s), 27, 28, 36, 55; 'dove', 129; Earliest Carvings, 28, 55–6; fleur(s)-de-lis, 35, 129; four-petal flower, 13; fox and two birds, 35, 78–88; graffiti, medieval, 59, 99; graffiti, modern, 17, 20, 130; hearts, 35, 91; horse(s), 28, 55, 129; hunter(s), 28, 55, 56; hunting dogs, 55; initials, 129, 130; knight's head, 28; lions/lion cubs, 28, 110; outline images, 13, 17–36; over-carved images, 17, 27, 28, 55, 56; ragged staff, 124, 127; re-discovered group of images, 56; runic letters, 129; scallops, 27, 28, 35, 123; '1603', 130, 135–6; stag(s), 36, 55; stag's head, 28; stick-like images, 13, 36; '1321', 35, 129, 135–6; Tudor rose, 27; unknown bearded face, 129–130; wheat sheaves, 130, 135; white hart, 17, 20; white Yorkist rose, 27

carver, the first, 39–40, 59

carving process, 18–19, 55

Cathedral of the Dales (St Stephen's Church, Kirkby Stephen), 88

Catherine's wheel, 27

Champion, Matthew, 100

changes to male images in Room 22 – 103–4

Church of St Peter in Pavia, 105

Clifford: George, 3rd Earl of Cumberland, 136; Robert de, 66 73

Clifford family, 69

Comyn (Lords of Badenoch and Lochaber): Johan, Sire, 135; John I, 'The Black Comyn', 135; John II, 'The Red Comyn', 92, 135

Council of Trent (Trento), 100

crucified man, 27, 91, 107

Crusades: against the Cathars (1209–29), instigated by Innocent III, 93–4; Reconquista of Southern Spain (1325 to 1340), led by King Alphonso XI of Castille and Leon, 93; to Egypt, 7th Crusade (1248–54), led by Louis IX of France, 93; to the Holy Land, 1st Crusade (1096), 92; to Tunis, 8th Crusade (1267), led by Louis IX, 93

Cumberland and Westmorland Antiquarian and Archaeological Society, 99

Cumbrian tales, 77–8

Dacre: Humphrey, 109, 117–18, 119; Randolf, 9th Baron Dacre of Gillesland, 109, 116–17; Ranulph, 1st Baron Dacre of Gillesland, 35–6, 66; Thomas, 1st Baron Dacre of Greystoke / 2nd Baron Dacre of Gillesland, 28, 69, 123;Thomas, 6th Baron Dacre of Gillesland, 127; William, 2nd Baron Dacre of Gillesland, 127

Dacre Beasts: 36, 55, 69–74, 109, 123; Bull, 36, 72–3, 123, 127; Dolphin, 36, 73–4, 84, 109; Gryphon, 36, 70–71, 109; Ram, 71–2

Dacre family, 69, 71, 72–73, 74, 123

Dacre knot, 109

Dacre Prickers, see *Border Light Horse and Lancers*

Dacre scallop, 27, 28, 35, 123

Douglas, Sir James, 'Good Sir James' / 'The Black Douglas', 35, 86, 91–6

Ebola virus, 107

Edmund Plantagenet, Duke of Rutland, 113

Edward of Westminster, Prince of Wales, 110, 115, 120

Emperors of Rome: Carinus, 104; Diocletian, 105; Maxentius, 27

Fauconberg, William, Lord Fauconberg (Duke of Warwick's uncle), 114

fetterlock, 96

F. J. Field, 84, 99

fox: 83, 84; and two birds, 35, 78–88; disguised fox, preaching to some birds, 84; Edward II as a fox, 88; Reynard the fox, 84

fox and geese, 78, 83

fox and hounds, 83
fox and sheep, 83

Jerusalem, 92, 94

Plantagenet, Geoffrey V, Count of Anjou (2nd husband of Matilda of England), 61

Platt, Colin, 99

Popes: Clement V, 92; Clement XIII, 103; Innocent III, 93–4; Innocent X, 103; John XXII, 92; Leo XIII, 103; Pius IV, 103; Pius IX, 103; Urban II, 92, 93

prayers in stone, 107

Queens: Catherine of Aragon, 123; Elizabeth I, 35, 130, 136; Margaret of Anjou, 110, 113–15, 118–19, 124; Mary of Guelders, 110, 113, 118; Mary Queen of Scots, 35, 136

Ragnar 'Hairy Breeches' Lodbrok, 104

Richard Plantagenet, Duke of York, Edward IV's father, 110, 113

Robert, 5th Lord of Annandale, 135

Room 22: door, 40, 55; East Wall, 20, 27, 28, 39, 40, 56; North Wall, 13, 20, 39, 40, 56, 99, 104, 107; South Wall, 20, 27, 28, 35, 36, 39, 40, 56, 91, 103, 109, 123; see also entries under *Carlisle Castle*

Roos: Henry, 109, 116, 119; Thomas, 10th Baron Roos of Hamlake, 109, 116, 119

Roos family badge, 13

saints: Catherine of Alexandria, 27; Edmund, 99, 104; George, 17, 20, 105; Irene of Rome, 105; Matilda of Ringelheim, 62; Sebastian, 99, 104–5, 107

Saladin, 94

Salkeld, Sir Richard, a Neville retainer and commander of the Carlisle garrison, 119

Salmon, 73–4, 84

saltire, 123, 127

Salvin, Anthony (restorer of the Dacre Beasts, 1849), 71

Saxton, 116–117

Scott, Sir Walter – his book *The Talisman*, 96

Scott, Walter, of Buccleuch, 129–30